RECYCLE YOUR GARDEN

CW01594225

Gardening Australia

RECYCLE YOUR GARDEN

TIM MARSHALL

ABC Books

In memory of Michael Bradley, who provided much support and encouragement for my busy and complex life during the preparation of this book.

Published by ABC Books for the
AUSTRALIAN BROADCASTING CORPORATION
GPO Box 9994 Sydney NSW 2001

Copyright © Australian Broadcasting Corporation 2003

First published April 2003

All rights reserved. No part of this publication may be reproduced, stored in a retrieval system or transmitted in any form or by any means, electronic, mechanical, photocopying, recording or otherwise, without the prior written permission of the Australian Broadcasting Corporation.

The ABC has made every effort to acknowledge copyright holders. Please direct details of any omissions to ABC Books, GPO Box 9994, Sydney 2001.

ISBN 0 7333 0984 4

Designed by and typeset by Mega City Design
Illustrations by Nives Porcellato and Andy Craig
All photographs by the author unless otherwise credited
Cover photographs by Jeff Dale and Tim Marshall
Set in Berkeley 11½/14pt
Colour reproduction by Pageset, Melbourne
Printed and bound in China by Everbest

Contents

Introduction

Composting is an easy, rewarding and profitable activity. Your garden will benefit and so will the environment, as you reuse organic matter, recycle nutrients and save on fuel and landfill space. The basic process of composting is simple: collect as much organic matter as possible at one time, pile it up loosely so that air can move into the heap, add enough water to thoroughly wet the heap, and let it rot. Good compost has the wonderful smell of forest soil and leaf litter. This rich, earthy-smelling humus is actually the product of rotted plants and animals. In finished compost no hint of the original material remains: only clean, soil-like organic matter.

There are also side benefits from composting. For example, as you develop enthusiasm for composting, the time spent pulling weeds becomes more meaningful. Now you have a use for those weeds after all. Weeding and composting have a natural synergy. Weeds feed the compost, compost applied as mulch improves the soil, and the weeds become easier to pull. Before long, you will notice an improvement in plant growth where compost has been used. The soil will be easier to dig, and weeds will come free with less effort.

Soil improvement in the organic garden is not limited to composting. *In situ* soil building is vital. This is achieved by minimising tillage, protecting the surface with mulch, and growing green manures. By staying away from chemical sprays and fertilisers, the natural organisms are given a fair go. If the whole garden is treated organically, and the soil improved with compost, after several seasons there will be a noticeable improvement in overall plant health. This means fewer pests and diseases, plus less watering. Seeing is believing, and experience will convince even the sceptics that organic growing is the most sensible way to go.

Enough is known about how soil works, and there are many organic farm and garden products available, to enable every soil to be managed organically. Virtually every pest can be treated by organic methods, and where they cannot, the disruption caused by strong chemicals is hardly worthwhile.

We all need time away from the bustle of life. What better way than gardening? The time spent close to the soil during weeding and composting expands the gardener's understanding of biodiversity and the need to make room for nature's complex processes, even in our cities and backyards. It is an awareness we must develop if we are to manage our land and water resources sustainably. So whether you look at it from an environmental, financial, health or philosophical view, composting makes good sense.

1. Introduction to composting

'One aker with compost
Is worth akers three
At harvest thy barne
Shall declare it to thee'
THOMAS TUSSER, 1557

Compost is the ultimate plant food and soil amendment. It is the secret to healthy soil and healthy plants. It improves soil structure, protects plants from pests and disease, builds soil fertility, and provides essential plant nutrients. Without a doubt, compost is unsurpassed as a soil and plant health product.

What is compost?

There are many definitions of compost. Typically, it is the product of the biological decomposition of organic wastes under the correct conditions. In nature, anything that once lived, or was produced by something that lived, is then decomposed by other living organisms. Grass cuttings, hay, a corncob from the table and a dead animal are examples of something that lived. Hair and dung are 'the product' of something that lived.

Compost is the ideal soil additive for organic growing because it works as a fertiliser, a soil conditioner and a biological inoculant. It is a fertiliser because it contains nutrients and it is a soil conditioner because it improves the soil's structure and its ability to hold water and recover from compaction. As a biological inoculant it adds many valuable organisms and their enzymatic or growth-stimulating by-products to soil. These compost organisms and their by-products continue to add value because they help soil to process its own organic wastes and combat soil-borne diseases.

Finished compost is dark in colour, moist, sweet smelling and colloidal. This latter term refers to its ability to hold water and nutrients. A colloid remains in suspension in water for a very long time, or indefinitely. For example, jelly crystals are colloids. They can absorb enormous quantities of water to form jelly, but it is not easy to squeeze water back out of them. Plant roots can extract water, and nutrients, from colloids.

The colloidal properties of compost can be roughly demonstrated by rolling it into a tight ball in your hands. Break it up, and then roll it again into a ball. This can be done repeatedly, without loss of crumb structure, because of the colloids. Good compost is also homogenous: it has uniform particles and colour, and almost none of the original ingredients are discernible.

I have been taking a sample of my best compost to gardening classes and compost workshops for years, demonstrating how it can be rolled into a smooth ball, not unlike plasticine, then broken down into crumbs. This is done repeatedly while talking to the class, then the sample is passed to the class and they do the same. The compost continues to roll into a ball and to break apart into crumbs. After years of use the sample still doesn't need replacing. Imagine what that sort of stability can do for your soil when it is under pressure from walking (or driving on farmland), irrigation or rainfall.

Compost and Australian soils

Most Australian soils in their native state probably contained 3–5 per cent organic matter. Organic matter is a generic term for plant and animal residues and soil organisms. The organic matter may be fresh, partly decomposed or completely decomposed. Under farming and cultivation, the organic matter level of Australian soil has dropped to less than 2 per cent. This has made the soil vulnerable to erosion and slowed down the rate at which nutrients can be cycled, captured and held in the soil. If organic matter levels fall low enough, even the use of conventional fertilisers cannot improve yields.

This fall in the amount of organic matter is already happening in some of the most historically productive farming areas.

Composting is a great way to make your own soil-improver. Compost is easily made at home, even in a small garden, or it can be purchased from local councils or 'green waste' recovery and composting companies. Compost is also relevant to farm soil management. Although organic and low-input broadacre farms rely on minimal tillage, cover crops, green manures and trash retention to develop soil organic matter *in situ*, large-scale composting of crop wastes is still an economic and practical option using readily available equipment, such as a forage harvester, front-end loader or rake.

The three Rs

Compost can also benefit the general environment. Reduce, reuse and recycle are three basic rules for ecological living. Carting rubbish to waste disposal sites takes time and money. Landfill space close to towns and cities is a declining resource. Instead of throwing away lawn clippings, kitchen scraps, pruning waste and even old papers, throw them in the compost.

Compost reduces the amount of garbage hauled to the rubbish dump. Homemade compost reduces the gardener's reliance on purchased products, including their expensive packaging and transport.

Compost adds value to waste materials from the garden and kitchen, or crop residue from farming by recycling nutrients back into the soil. Importantly, composting also keeps the nutrients out of waterways and oceans.

Compost as a soil conditioner

As a physical conditioner of soil, compost just can't be beaten. The humus that compost provides helps alleviate all significant soil problems and improves soil structure, strength, erosion resistance and permeability. Compost helps soils:

- retain more moisture
- recover more rapidly from trauma caused by wheel and foot traffic or cultivation
- provide easier passage for earthworms and plant roots
- insulate roots from temperature extremes.

Compost also helps to moderate high and low pH in soils.

Compost as a biological inoculant

As a biological inoculant, compost adds live beneficial organisms: food for microbes and enzymes, which stimulate their growth. Many garden and agricultural soils desperately need compost as a source of the diverse biological components that have been depleted by years of cultivation, bare fallow and the use of chemical fertilisers and pesticides.

Compost and soil nutrition

Many older books on composting underestimated the value of compost as a fertiliser. They stressed the importance of compost as a soil amendment but ignored its other functions. The analysis the authors used was probably based on municipal compost, or on compost made from only a few sources of raw material.

If a great variety of raw materials are used the resulting compost can be a useful nutritional benefit. Of course, compost doesn't have the final nutrient concentration of bagged fertiliser, but as much larger quantities of compost are used, significant fertility improvements do result from applying compost and mulch. Compost provides other critical benefits that artificial nutrients cannot. If plants show a nutrient deficiency it may still be useful to apply certified organic mineral fertilisers and blood and bone, or liquid seaweed and fish fertiliser. Many organic gardens thrive on small additions of these concentrated products, if the soil is kept in good health by the use of compost and mulch.

A variety of certified organic crushed natural rock fertilisers, waste by-products (for example, blood and bone), composted fertiliser products and liquid preparations are readily available through local garden centres, by mail order, or from fertiliser suppliers listed under 'organic' in the phone book.

Compost also helps to release nutrients that have been tied up in the soil. By improving soil structure, compost allows better leaching of undesirable salts, which damage soil fertility.

The compost recipe

Making good compost is like baking a cake. First you assemble the ingredients, then you mix them together, including air

Benefits of compost

- improves the ability of soil to absorb water
- reduces run-off
- increases moisture-holding capacity of soil
- provides food for beneficial soil organisms, such as worms
- helps to suppress harmful soil organisms, such as nematodes
- supplies nutrients in a slow-release form
- supplies the full range of macro-nutrients and trace elements
- helps to hold nutrients in the soil and prevent leaching
- reduces fertiliser requirements
- buffers soil pH and increases plant tolerance to acid or alkaline conditions
- stimulates the production of vitamins, growth hormones and other growth-stimulating substances
- maintains good aeration in soil, which helps water penetration
- improves the structure and drainage of all soils, including sand or clay
- reduces soil erosion
- keeps soil cool in summer and warm in winter
- assists with lock-up of toxic substances, such as pesticides or heavy metals, keeping them safely away from plant roots.

into the mix, then you 'bake' it until 'cooked'. It's best not to eat the compost!

The recipe includes:

Carbon and nitrogen materials These elements are food for micro-organisms. There should be enough mass of material to produce high temperatures.

Micro-organisms In practice there are enough micro-organisms present in any soil, and compost made direct on the soil or with ingredients that have been stored on the soil should have enough to work. If in doubt, add a compost activator.

Moisture The material should be damp but not saturated. It should not be possible to squeeze free moisture out of the heap.

Air If moisture levels are correct, and you have not trodden on or otherwise compacted the heap, trapped air will be sufficient to start with. Over time, as the heap collapses, air is excluded, unless it is replenished by use of aerating holes or turning the heap.

Time The other essential component in the recipe is time. A good heap in ideal conditions during summer takes at least seven or eight weeks, if turned several times. The process may take much longer in winter, or if the heap is not turned, or the carbon to nitrogen mix is not right.

A sense of humus

Humus is dark in colour, smells like sweet earth, is gummy, colloidal and has very high water-holding capacity. Humus is made by soil organisms, especially fungi and bacteria, and by slow breakdown of plant parts containing lignin, which does not decompose readily. These products, reworked over and over again by many soil organisms, interact with each other to form humus.

Depending on the composition of the raw materials, the particular bacteria and fungi involved and the balance between bacterial and fungal activity, and soil conditions such as moisture, temperature and aeration, the characteristics of humus can vary. There are many different types of humus, and all humus is subtly unique.

Humus provides the following functions:

Water retention Humus can hold up to one hundred times its own weight in water.

Nutrient holding Humus holds nutrients in the soil and protects them from leaching or erosion, but in a form accessible to plants.

Improves soil structure Humus has an open, lattice structure that holds air and water. Humus makes soils lighter to work and helps to gum individual soil particles together into aggregates or crumbs, permitting easier entry of water, air and plant roots. It improves sandy and clay soils equally well.

Helps soil to warm Because it is dark in colour and holds air, which has an insulating capacity, humus modifies extreme soil temperatures.

Balanced pH Humus provides a buffering function that helps bring both acid and alkaline soils back to a balanced pH.

Immobilises contaminants Humus can hold soil contaminants such as lead, cadmium and pesticide residues, preventing them from entering plants and hence the food chain.

Feeds the soil food web Humus is made by soil life and is consumed and broken down by soil life. Humus is continually being made and destroyed in a healthy soil ecosystem.

Organic soil management

Good practices

- Spend time observing in the garden. Learn the natural cycles, and catch weeds, pests and diseases before they have the opportunity to spread.
- Crop rotation reduces demands on nutrient cycling and soil structure, and helps control weed, pest and disease cycles.
- Flowers and shrubs provide habitat for beneficial insects, so plant them near productive areas.
- Use ponds, rock heaps, bird boxes and refuge areas to provide habitat for lizards, birds and other beneficial organisms.
- Green manures are a good way to rejuvenate soil. Use them between flower and vegetable crops, or over the winter.
- Keep soil covered as much as possible with a good organic mulch.
- Use compost and raw organic matter on the soil surface to smother weeds and improve structure.

Undesirable practices

- Don't leave soil bare or exposed more than necessary, especially over the winter.
- Don't put prunings and vegetable waste into the garbage bin: doing so is expensive and wasteful.
- Avoid growing large areas of monoculture, or the same crop year after year, in the same patch.
- Burning autumn leaves and other organic waste pollutes the atmosphere and causes nutrient loss.
- Turning soil too often, or always at the same depth, creates hard pans and destroys soil structure.
- Don't use chemicals that can harm beneficial insects in the soil or on plants. Not all insects and other animals are pests. They could be your best allies for pest and disease control.
- Don't use herbicides because they damage soil organisms and interfere with natural soil ecosystems.

2. The 'basic' compost method

'Composting is a fascinating game that grows on you'
LADY EVE BALFOUR, *THE LIVING SOIL*, 1943

The simple aerobic composting method described in this chapter is an easy, foolproof method for any garden with enough space to devote a small area to composting. Inexperienced compost-makers would do well to succeed with this simple method before experimenting with other techniques. Fortunately the process is quite forgiving, and a novice can expect some early success from the simple guidelines.

The breakdown of organic matter

All organic matter can be composted. Organic matter is anything that was once alive, or the product of anything that once lived. Vegetable waste, hair, sawdust, manure, urine, straw, tea leaves and coffee grounds are examples of products suitable for composting. Some types of organic matter, such as meat waste and pine needles can be composted, but require special treatment because of possible problems with disease, high pH or antagonistic chemicals. To avoid problems, these products should only be used in small amounts by the novice composter. Meat and fish waste should only be used by very experienced composters, as they can cause hygiene and community health problems. Using more than small quantities of these products may require a licence or approval from public health or environmental agencies.

In nature all organic waste is broken down, usually at or near the soil surface, by various micro-organisms. In certain conditions, large amounts of organic matter can collect together, perhaps blown against a fallen log in a forest. Here the heat produced by the metabolism (body heat) of millions of compost micro-organisms is retained by the layers of insulating organic matter, and breakdown processes are greatly accelerated. The efficiency of these organisms is greater at higher temperatures, and if air and water are available their rapid rate of increase continues as long as food sources remain. It is this natural process which is imitated in the compost heap.

The main micro-organisms involved are bacteria, fungi and actinomycetes. Fungi include mushrooms, moulds, rusts and yeast. Fungi and actinomycetes make filament-like growth, but actinomycetes are more closely related to bacteria. These organisms dominate different stages of decay in the heap. Larger organisms such as worms, slaters and millipedes are also active as the heap cools down. The first effect on the organic matter is chemical breakdown from within, caused by internal heat and the actions of enzymes within individual cells that are still living. Soon after, bacteria begin to decompose the particles, starting work on the surface. Smaller particles have a greater surface area, leading to more rapid breakdown by bacteria.

Build the heap on soil

Home composters should never build a compost heap on concrete. Direct contact with soil allows micro-organisms to move into the heap. More importantly, building the heap on soil allows earthworms and other larger creatures to move into the heap and escape back into the soil when the temperature of the heap rises.

Some commercial compost heaps are built on a concrete slab, but they are closely monitored by professional managers, and generally serviced by specialised equipment to introduce air and compost organisms.

Use smallest particles

If possible, reduce the size of raw material particles before composting. Use a shredder or chipper, or improvise by running the mower over the weeds and other waste to reduce particle size. Tough stalks, such as maize stems, are easily broken into shorter lengths by hand. If particle size can't be reduced, the heap will still work, but breakdown of material will be slower.

Controlling the carbon to nitrogen ratio

The micro-organisms at work in the compost heap have their own dietary needs, just as people do. They require 25 units of carbon for every unit of nitrogen (called the C:N ratio). Maintaining this ratio is easier than you might think, and simple instructions follow later in the book. Fortunately the process will still work if the C:N ratio is a little out of balance. The compost may take longer to finish, and the final nutrient value may be a little less. Remember too that micro-organisms require trace elements. The best way to provide these is to use a wide variety of different raw materials in the heap. For the C:N ratio of some commonly available materials, refer to the table in Chapter 3.

The actual nutrient values of these materials will depend on how healthy the plants were, the feed source for animals, and how fresh the material is. Older manure will lose nitrogen and some other elements to the atmosphere or from leaching. The presence of suitable bedding, such as sawdust or straw, will reduce the rate of loss.

Use a variety of materials

A variety of materials ensures that there is a wide range of nutrients in the finished product and helps to restrict the limiting effects of difficult materials. For instance, the tough structure and acidity of pine needles is balanced by mixing with softer, sappier materials, such as leaves, lawn clippings, kitchen waste, hay, horse manure and weeds. A good rule of thumb is to use at least three different materials and to use no single material for more than about one-third of the heap. The only exception to this guideline may be weeds or other recently harvested plant material if they are fresh, succulent and healthy.

One cubic metre or more

Temperature is important to the heap and regulates the activity of the organisms involved. As the outside of the heap insulates the interior against heat loss, a certain minimum size is necessary. The ratio of surface area to volume is greater for a smaller heap, so heat is lost more quickly from a small heap. The process works best in a very large heap where temperature does not drop below the minimum requirement and the 'thermophilic' or hot stage lasts for as long as possible.

The heap should be at least 1 cubic metre in size. Large amounts of material can be composted in a long windrow, at least a metre high by a metre wide by any length longer than a metre. Don't build a smaller heap. If there isn't enough material on hand, there are five choices:

1 Use a plastic compost bin (this is an anaerobic compost, a different process, and is described in Chapter 9).
2 Store the various ingredients separately until you have enough to put them together to construct the heap.
3 Build the heap in stages over time, but this should not take more than four weeks and may be wasteful of nutrients, especially nitrogen.
4 Feed the material to compost worms in a worm farm.
5 Feed the material to chickens, rabbits or guinea pigs and collect their manure and bedding for compost later.

Let the air in

All the organisms involved in the processes described in this chapter are aerobic, meaning they need oxygen. A heap with a height or width greater than 2 or 2.5 metres may not allow enough oxygen into the middle.

Air channels need to be created in larger heaps. An easy way is to place long poles into the centre during construction. As the heap matures it collapses onto itself, forcing air out, and shrinking. When this happens, the poles can be carefully pulled out, leaving a clean hole straight into the centre. Plastic conduit with holes drilled into it can be used in the same way, although the heat from the compost destroys the plastic fairly quickly.

Never jump or walk on the heap, as this forces out air. Turning the heap reintroduces air. Turn the heap every week, or when it begins to cool, until the heap no longer reheats after turning. It can then be left to mature.

As the heap heats up, the higher temperatures kill most weed seeds and disease-causing organisms. Experienced compost-makers can safely compost most plant materials, but the novice is wise to exclude diseased plants and weed seeds. Turning the heap helps to make sure that all material spends some time in the hottest part at the core.

A variety of construction methods can be used, including a freestanding heap. Using bales of straw to contain the compost has several simple advantages:

- the heap is insulated by the bales and heat is retained
- compost is contained away from chickens or other animals that might spread it around
- the bales form a refuge for worms which escape the heap when the highest temperatures are reached
- it looks neater than a freestanding heap
- after one or two years in the compost system the bales are riddled with worm castings and make excellent mulch for a no-dig garden, or become part of a compost heap themselves.

Do not add lime

The correct pH is critical for the heap. The letters pH refer to a measure of acidity or alkalinity. Most bacteria prefer a pH of 6.0–7.5. Fungi tolerate a pH of 5.5–8.0. Generally, the heap should be left to its own devices. It may become acid during the early stages, but this is a natural process. The heap will adjust its own pH as the composting process continues and the finished product is usually around neutral, or pH 7.0.

Lime is a fine product for use on soil but put it there rather than in the compost. The solubility of nitrogen is increased at high pH and this valuable element will be leached or volatilised (evaporated) from the heap if lime is added. Many otherwise reputable books on the subject incorrectly advise the addition of lime. An exception is when large quantities of sugar or starch (such as fruit waste, which can be quite acid) are used in a heap.

Damp but not wet

Water is the other essential composting ingredient. Too much water will displace oxygen from the spaces between particles and slow down composting. If the bottom of the heap has free water, turn it to dry the heap out. If it is very wet, turn it over a period of several hours on a warm day, leaving the middle exposed. If there is too little water, a dry white powder may rise from the heap when it is opened up. This indicates that fungi and actinomycetes have stopped working, and are moving into a dormant, spore-producing stage.

Think of the moisture requirement as a squeezed out sponge: thoroughly damp but will not yield water when wrung. In this condition the heap will contain between 40–60 per cent water.

Cover the heap

If the heap is exposed to the weather it may become too wet or too dry. Cover it with hessian sacks or cloth, old blankets, carpet squares or thick packing cardboard. The best cover of all is a solid roof elevated above the heap, to shed rainwater and provide shade without limiting air movement in and out of the heap.

If black plastic or other impervious materials are used to cover the heap, place

pH: the acid test

The pH scale is a measure of acidity or alkalinity. A pH of 0 is pure acid, 14.0 is pure base, or alkaline. A pH of 7.0 is neutral. The scale is a logarithmic progression: an increase of 1 unit indicates a 10 times increase in acidity. Compost bacteria prefer a pH value of 6.0–7.0. The first few days of a compost heap may produce acid conditions. This could persist for the first few weeks. The pH generally self-adjusts back to neutral as the heap matures.

You can measure pH with a simple test kit. Kits that use a combination of a powder reagent and liquid dye are most reliable for home use. Paper pH test ribbon and pH meters are less reliable.

Acid	
0	battery acid
1	weak hydrochloric acid
2	lemon juice, vinegar
3	orange juice
4	acid rain
5	cow's milk
6	saliva
Neutral	
7	Distilled water, human blood
Alkaline	
8	seawater
9	baking soda
10	milk of magnesia
11	ammonia (NH_3)
12	bleach solution
13	bleach (undiluted), oven cleaner
14	caustic soda

timbers under the plastic sheet to create an air gap to allow the heap to keep breathing.

Keep trying

The benefits of well-made compost are so great, it is worth persisting if results from early attempts are not all that you had hoped for. Compost really is the best tool the organic grower has. As well as basic garden compost, special composts can be made for various purposes, including leaf mould for potting and disease-control composts for spraying onto plants or watering into the root zone.

The method described in this chapter will make good compost. Some gardeners claim improvements can be made to the system by adding special compost preparations or herbs, but perfectly satisfactory compost is easily made from readily available materials. In reality, the best compost starter is cheap and simple: a little of the previous compost worked back through the new heap.

Avoid pests and diseases

Beware when bringing any material onto the farm or into the garden. Avoid doing so if possible. The material may contain weed seeds, pesticides or other contaminants. When buying in composting ingredients, try to establish that all materials are clean. Seaweed, straw and animal manures are some of the easiest to obtain. Check local regulations before collecting seaweed. Most local councils permit some collection for home use. Correct composting will help to ensure the safety of these materials too.

Most of the hormones or antibiotics found in manures will be broken down at temperatures reached during efficient aerobic composting. The heat and biological processes within the heap will also break down some pesticides. However, some pesticides and all heavy metals can be concentrated in the finished product. If one material is a major input into the compost, it could be worthwhile testing it for pesticide residues.

3. How composting works

'Simply stated, composting is the biological decomposition of the organic constituents of wastes under controlled conditions.'
CLARENCE S. GOLUEKE, 1972

There are many influences on the development of a compost heap. Some important factors are the nutrient content (especially the C:N ratio) of the organic matter, air and moisture content, ambient temperature and the particular types and varieties of compost organisms present. The progress of the heap in ideal conditions is fairly predictable. The cause of any failures is generally fairly easy to discover too. Refer to pages 80–81 for hints on how to diagnose problems in the compost heap.

What happens inside the heap?

If air, water and nutrients are adequate, the heap will generally heat up quickly, within ten hours in summer and 24 hours in winter. Any obnoxious smells from manures or food waste should be totally gone by this time. The metabolising of bacteria, as they busily decompose the organic wastes and rapidly divide to increase their population, causes the heating of the heap at this stage.

The heap will quickly reduce in volume as the green wastes decompose. This size reduction causes the heap to collapse, forcing some air out of the heap. Following this, the process may slow due to lack of oxygen, unless adequate air passages remain.

The heap stays very hot for about five days before beginning to cool. It will be totally cool several weeks later, unless turned to aerate. A number of fungi start to work while the heap is still hot. After some cooling, other fungi and actinomycetes take over.

If the heap is turned when it begins to cool, the hot composting stage can be prolonged. This is considered desirable because the high temperatures help to sterilise the heap, and because a fine, crumbly end-product is available to use quicker. After about five to six weeks, if the heap is turned it will no longer reheat, even in summer.

The heap is now cool, but has not finished working. Compost micro-organisms are still at work, and at this stage worms, slaters, millipedes and other larger animals can move in too. They will process and reprocess the residues, until it is a dark-coloured, sweet-smelling, soil-like mass. At this stage the heap looks homogenous, which means there is very little sign of the original material. Here and there the shape of a leaf may remain, with the veins still visible. If picked up and rubbed gently between the fingers, the leaf totally disappears into black sticky material.

The heap has been successful. It has produced humus, the final product of decomposition and undeniably the best universal addition to any productive soil.

The heap will continue to reduce in volume and form a more concentrated product, but some of the goodness may leach out if the heap isn't stored well. Compost can be used as mulch at any time, but is best to leave it until it has become a homogenous, dark-coloured, soil-like mass.

Inside the heap, organic materials have been broken down to simple constituents by bacteria. Carbohydrates — sugars and starches — are quickly broken down to very simple short-chain sugars, organic acids and carbon dioxide. Proteins decompose to peptides and amino acids, which then continue to break down to ammonium and eventually plant-available nitrogen. Some resistant materials take longer to decompose; fungi and actinomycetes continue working on them.

The wastes and dead, or live, bodies of the composting organisms are consumed by other organisms. The next feeding level of organisms are preyed on and their wastes are decomposed by yet another set of organisms. A whole ecosystem is at work, with a food chain as complex as a forest. Before humus is produced, all the organic matter will have been processed and reprocessed many times.

It is easier to manage the composting process with a little knowledge. The physics and chemistry of the heap are fascinating and complex. Here, they are simply explained.

Air

Oxygen is essential for good open heap or windrow composting. The organisms that drive the aerobic composting process need oxygen to survive. To ensure good airflow into compost:

- Keep the heap lower or narrower than 2.5m — the third dimension can be as large as necessary, to form a long windrow.
- Pile the heap loosely. Never walk on the compost, and apply water carefully to avoid compaction.
- Use airholes. They can be made by using plastic conduit with holes, which may bend and collapse in very hot compost, or by placing poles in the heap when it is being made that can be carefully pulled out to leave airholes into the middle of the heap. This technique is very good, and surprisingly large, neat holes will survive in the heap if the pole has smooth sides that allow it to be pulled out without snagging bits of compost. The holes will persist for some time if you don't collapse them by walking over the heap. Some people drive a garden stake or crowbar into the heap and work it around to make a small hole. If you use this technique, try to avoid compaction immediately around the hole, by working the stake in and out, as well as around.
- Turn the heap and pile it loosely in a new spot.
- A good compost pile will heat to 55°C within twelve to 24 hours of being made. After a while the heap will collapse onto itself, forcing air out. Lack of oxygen becomes limiting at this stage, the process slows down and the heap cools. The heap should be turned to reheat if you wish to make the fastest, high-value compost.

Even inside a large, well-constructed heap there may be pockets that do not receive sufficient air. In these locations, anaerobic bacteria will multiply. They still make useful compost, but they may manufacture sulphur-containing chemicals that smell like rotten eggs or ammonia.

Many books recommend a layer of dry brush under the compost to encourage air into the heap. If you don't turn the heap, this could be a useful practice, but composters who turn the heap find the brush tangles in the tines of the turning tool. If the heap doesn't sit on the soil, you may also have to use a compost starter. Inevitably, as the compost matures, fine material works down through the brush, and the brush becomes part of the heap, to be sieved out later. I recommend the following ways to get air into a heap.

The airhole Airholes are made by thrusting a crowbar or tomato stake into the heap, which can be physically demanding if there are large weeds and fibrous particles. It will also cause compaction around the hole unless done carefully.

The periscope In this system a piece of plastic conduit or slotted agricultural drain is buried into the heap. Holes are drilled in the conduit, so that air can move into the heap. After several uses, the conduit may melt and collapse as a result of compost heat.

The straw tunnel This system works well for compost that will be left to mature with no turning. Straw 'biscuits' are broken off the bale and leaned up to form an inverted V shape, with a gap down the middle. Compost is then carefully laid over the top. The straw will decompose slower than the rest of the heap, because of its high C:N ratio, and will continue to allow some air movement into the bottom and centre of the heap.

Moisture

Compost should contain 40–60 per cent moisture. Like a wrung-out sponge, all the material should feel wet, but it should not be possible to squeeze free water from it. If the moisture level is ideal, the material will glisten a little with wetness.

The internal heat of the heap drives moisture off, and especially in summer extra moisture will need to be added from time to time. Stick a probe into the heap occasionally to monitor moisture levels, or examine the compost when turning the heap. If any material feels dry, add more water.

If the piled organic matter gets too dry it may be hard to re-wet. If this happens, put the water on slowly with a low-volume sprinkler or turn the sprinkler on for ten minutes every hour, or use a soaker hose over a windrow. If the pile gets really dry, add diluted liquid seaweed as a wetting agent.

When wetting dry straw to make a new compost heap, remember that it is capable of holding ten times its weight in water but it sheds water easily. To help wet such dry materials as straw, add a little liquid seaweed to a watering can and sprinkle over the straw, or add liquid seaweed to a bath or bucket of water in which the straw can be left to soak.

If the raw material is dry, always wet it during the building of the heap. Don't wait until the heap is made because it will shed water, and water may flow through the heap in rivers or channels, leaving other parts of the heap dry.

Too much moisture excludes air from the heap and slows the composting process. This favours anaerobic organisms, which may produce unpleasant smells. Dank compost can also harbour unpleasant organisms, such as *Legionella*, *Listeria* or *E. coli*. Prevent the heap from becoming waterlogged with an external layer of straw, or cover with a plastic sheet during rainy periods.

Carbon to nitrogen ratio

The carbon to nitrogen (C:N) ratio is the measure of carbon and nitrogen content of raw materials. Research indicates that there is an ideal ratio, based on the dietary requirement of compost micro-organisms. The ideal ratio is 25 to 30 parts of carbon to one part of nitrogen. There is no need to be precise but designing the heap to be close to these levels will speed the composting process and ensure that nutrients are efficiently used, and that, other conditions being suitable, good heat can develop which will aid seed and disease kill.

As a general rule, actively growing, healthy and succulent plants will already contain a suitable C:N ratio for composting. A heap made only of fresh, actively growing plant materials will have adequate or excess nitrogen. If legumes such as clovers or pea straw, or significant quantities of kitchen waste are included, there will be sufficient nitrogen to mix in up to one-third carbonaceous materials, such as dry leaves or shredded paper.

Temperature

Temperature is a key factor for successful composting and the key single indicator of successful progress of the composting process. Factors affecting temperature include:

- compost ingredients, including C:N ratio, particle size and moisture content
- size and shape of the compost heap, which affects aeration and the insulation/radiation balance of the compost
- ambient temperature, which affects compost temperatures and rate of heat loss.

The ideal fast-composting method generates significant heat within about ten hours of constructing the heap. At different temperatures, different species of bacteria will take over. They go dormant at unfavourable temperatures but there are many different types, adapted to working at lesser or greater heat levels. To maintain ideal internal temperatures for long enough:

- build the heap to at least 1 cubic metre — 1.5 cubic metres or bigger is better
- insulate the heap with an outer layer of straw or soil, or
- build the compost in a bin made from insulating materials.

Eventually the heap will cool and it will not be possible to reheat it unless new material is added. This is the right time to stop turning the heap and let it sit to mature.

Temperature of the heap can be tested with a thermometer. There are simple digital remote thermometers available with a short lead that can be dangled into a hole in the compost, made with a crowbar

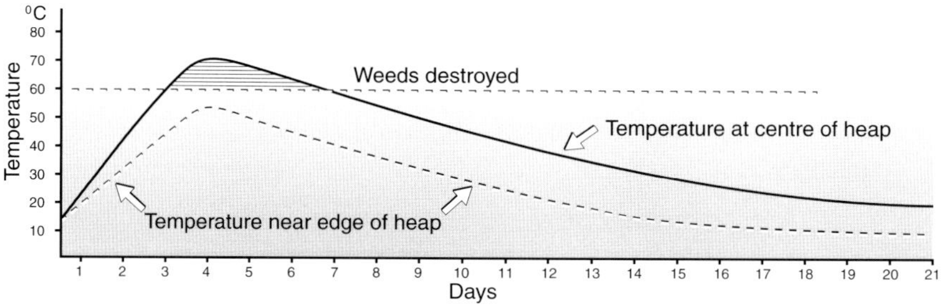

Compost heap temperature

Nitrogen content and C:N ratio of various compost ingredients

Material	C:N ratio (weight basis)	Nitrogen content (% dry weight)
Blood	3:1	16–18
Cow manure	12:1	1.8–2.3
Fish waste	7:1	6.5–12
Horse manure	12:1	2–4
Kitchen waste	15:1	3–7
Lawn clippings (during growing season)	18–21:1	2–2.4
Newspaper	170–280:1	0.2
Oaten straw	45–60:1	1
Pig manure	–	2.3–2.9
Poultry manure (no sawdust)	6.5:1	6.5–7
Poultry manure (with sawdust)	9–11:1	4–5
Rabbit manure	2.4–6.5	–
Sawdust (raw)	450–520:1	0.1
Sawdust (rotted)	200:1	0.2–0.4
Sheep manure	0.7–1.1	
Urine	–	16–18
Weeds (growing season)	18–20:1	1.3–2.0
Wheat straw	120–130:1	0.3

Note: This table has been constructed by comparing analysis from various sources. Where a range of values is given, the higher value relates to better quality of animal feed, lower percentage of litter in manure, or organic matter harvested during peak growing periods. All nitrogen values will diminish with increasing storage time.

or tomato stake. An experienced composter can leave the crowbar thrust into the heap for several hours, and then pull it out to feel the internal temperature. The bar may become so hot that it is very difficult to grip the metal with a bare hand, a good indication that all is well in the centre of the pile.

The ambient air temperature will affect compost. The process will inevitably take longer in winter, and a shorter time in summer.

Maintaining a high temperature within the heap helps to kill any pathogens (disease-causing organisms) present in the heap. Some books say this sterilises the heap, but this is really an incorrect use of the word because a compost heap is a seething mass containing many billions of bacteria, fungi and other organisms, perhaps many hundreds of different types. Compost is not sterile, and some of the micro-organisms may be harmful, so don't eat compost and try not to inhale compost fumes or particles when turning the heap. A simple dust mask provides adequate protection.

Unless kept too dry, or too wet, or made from unsavoury protein-rich wastes, compost is generally quite safe to handle. The heat and competition or predation from beneficial organisms keeps pathogen levels very low. If good hot compost is made, most weed seeds and disease organisms will be controlled. Temperature is the key, and is the sole reason why composting may be preferred to worm farming for the disposal of some organic wastes. This means raising the temperature to 55°C and keeping it there for about five to seven days, then reforming the heap so the outside forms the core of a new heap, which also reheats to 55°C, for five days. The heap will continue to benefit from turning, up to the point where it will no longer reheat.

If the heap has cooled after five days it is ready for turning, but little will be lost if it is left for a while, until the weekend perhaps. For many home gardeners, the weekend will be the ideal time to turn the heap. The process will restart when the heap is turned, and only a few days of production time will be lost. Indeed, the heap will reheat if you miss a weekend and turn it on the next, but the time to completion is lengthened. It is better to keep the bacterial population explosion active because their bodies become part of the process, feeding the next layer in the food chain. This helps to maintain the heat in the heap.

Some seed may survive the composting process. Many organic gardens share the same weeds — tomatoes and pumpkins — as these seeds are very heat resistant. If you have to have weeds, these two are not a bad choice.

Although many pathogens are killed, some pathogens are also heat resistant. Novice composters would do well to burn or dump infected plants until they have mastered the composting process.

The 'hot' stage in composting is known as the thermophilic stage. Organisms active during this stage tolerate temperature ranges of 40–65°C.

After the thermophilic phase, mesophilic micro-organisms take over the decomposition. This is the cool, or mesophilic stage, during which compost no longer reheats if turned. Organisms active during this stage become dormant if temperatures rise too high and activate again when temperatures fall back to 40°C. They work best in the range 20–40°C. Compost temperature stays close to ambient conditions during this phase, but important processing is still occurring. Some composters use their product at this stage, and miss out on the benefits of mature compost. Think of this stage as a curing phase. Chemical reactions and physical changes that affect organic matter and developing humus continue to occur in the heap. These changes make humus more stable, longer lasting, remove any possibility of harm to plant roots and generally make it more suitable for use with any plants.

Bulding on soil, not concrete

The high temperatures reached in a well-built heap are an important reason why compost should be built on soil, not concrete. Invertebrates in the compost system survive the high temperature phase by moving into the soil or to the edge of the pile.

Regulating heat loss

The temperature of the compost depends on how much heat is produced by compost micro-organisms and how much is being lost through conduction, convection and radiation.

Conduction transfers energy by direct contact at the edges of the compost heap, causing heat loss to the air.

Convection transfers heat by movement of air or water. When compost reaches high temperatures, warm air rises from deep in the heap, setting up a convective current. Natural convection pulls air in from the bottom of the heap. Solid sides on compost containers, such as corrugated iron, can limit air intake. The sides may keep the heap vertical, but with careful stacking a freestanding heap can look better than untidy iron. If you do use iron sides, punch a few holes down low to facilitate convection. Some compost may trickle out, but vital air will find its way in. Some commercial composting systems use forced air powered by large blowers or fans.

Radiation refers to the gradual transfer of heat from the compost pile to the cooler surrounding air by electromagnetic waves. The warm glow you feel when standing in the sunlight or near a radiator or wood fire is due to radiation.

Most of the energy transferred is in the form of latent heat released when water evaporates. The steam rising from hot compost early in the morning is water vapour driven off by the internal heat of the pile. Moisture content affects temperature of the compost heap because water has a higher specific heat than most other compost ingredients. A compost heap that is dry will tend to heat up and cool down quicker than a wetter heap, if moisture levels remain adequate for microbial growth. If moisture levels fall too low, the composting process will slow down or stop altogether. Alternatively, very wet heaps are slow to heat up in winter or early spring.

The smaller the compost pile, the greater the surface area to volume ratio, and therefore the greater the degree of heat loss by conduction and radiation. Insulation provided by the outer layers of the heap in larger heaps, or by bin construction materials in small compost piles, will help to reduce heat losses.

Compost pH

The pH of most compost heaps should be left to itself. Some older books recommend addition of lime to the compost heap, but this is not advisable because nitrogen is more easily leached or lost to the atmosphere when lime is used. The compost initially becomes acidic, but over time the heap will settle out to finish at a slightly alkaline pH. In fact, most bacteria at work in the heap prefer a slightly alkaline environment, and fungi prefer a range from pH 5.5 to approximately pH 7.8.

Add lime to the soil, rather than to the compost heap. The exceptions to this rule are when making anaerobic composts (in plastic bins with a lid) or when compost is largely made from fruit waste or other very acidic materials.

Compost organisms

Organic residues provide the energy source for a wide range of compost organisms.

Primary consumers (organisms that eat organic residues) include bacteria, fungi, actinomycetes, nematodes, some types of mites, snails, slugs, earthworms and millipedes.

Secondary consumers (organisms that eat primary consumers) include springtails, some mites, beetles, nematodes and protozoa.

Tertiary consumers (organisms that eat secondary consumers) include centipedes, predatory mites, ground beetles, spiders and ants.

Bacteria in the centre of the heap break down organic residues. At the cooler edges, residues eaten by invertebrates such as millipedes, earthworms, snails and slugs, which shred the material, increase the surface area on which the micro-organisms can work. Micro-organisms are eaten by mites, springtails and other organisms, to form a complex ecosystem.

Bacteria

Three types of bacteria are involved in the compost process. Initially, psychrophilic bacteria proliferate, then mesophilic bacteria, and later, thermophilic bacteria dominate.

Psychrophylic bacteria are active in the heap when the temperature is below about 14°C, when the heap is first built. When the heat increases to 15–38°C, the mesophilic bacteria become active in the heap. Mesophilic bacteria keep the heap working, and generate their own metabolic heat. The temperature of the heap continues to increase, until eventually conditions become too hot for the mesophiles to continue decomposing. From a temperature of about 40–77°C, thermophilic bacteria will continue the composting work.

Bacteria reproduce at amazing speed. When the compost system is working well, they can double their population every 20 to 30 minutes. To get really fast, hot compost, you must utilise fast-working thermophilic bacteria. When food and water run short, or the temperature gets too high, even the thermophilic bacteria are killed, or slow down their activity. When the pile begins to cool off it should be turned, so that the centre of the heap is able to reheat and rekindle the fast-feeding and breeding activity of the thermophilic bacteria. If the heap is not turned, mesophilic bacteria take over again.

Compost can be made without turning, but fast compost is considered to be the best end-product, and is safer, because seeds and diseases will have been killed. If you don't need the fastest compost, refrain from turning the heap and let the mesophilic bacteria continue their work.

Eventually, the heap will no longer be able to retain enough heat to remain above 40°C, and there is no point in continuing to turn the heap further after this point. Just let the mesophilic bacteria take over again — they have been working away at the cooler outer layers all along. Other micro-organisms, fungi, protozoans and larger invertebrate compost animals will also start working effectively at this stage.

Fungi

Compost fungi can break down tough, debris-like cellulose into material that bacteria can decompose. Fungi can attack residues that are too dry, acidic, or low in nitrogen for bacteria. Most compost fungi are saprophytes, which live on the energy contained in dead or dying material.

There could be 1,000–5,000m of fungal hyphae (thin, thread-like fungal growth) per gram of good soil, and even more in compost. The extensive hyphae system is very good at extracting nutrients.

Fungi are active in the production of humic acids, which give soil or compost the familiar rich dark brown colour. They are eaten in the compost by nematodes, amoebae and some arthropods. Fungi and actinomycetes dominate during the final stages of composting, when the heap has cooled down.

Actinomycetes

The spider-web-like grey threads that invade maturing compost and the characteristic earthy smell of soil are caused by actinomycetes. Actinomycetes are important because the enzymes they produce can break down tough woody debris such as stems and bark, and newspaper.

Protozoa

Protozoa are one-celled microscopic animals that help to maintain plant-available nitrogen by feeding on bacteria. A good, maturing compost may contain 100,000 protozoa per gram. Fully mature compost and good soil may contain 100 to 10,000 protozoa per gram.

Nematodes

Nematodes are microscopic, worm-like creatures. They are one of the most widespread groups of animals and exist in nearly every habitat. Some nematodes are parasites of animals, including humans. Soil-dwelling nematodes that are active in compost eat bacteria, fungi, algae, yeasts, small invertebrates and other nematodes.

Nematodes do not like heat or anaerobic conditions. Fortunately, beneficial nematodes are more heat tolerant than the plant-feeders, so they can survive composting and surface exposure. Hot, aerobic composting kills harmful nematodes.

Invertebrates

Invertebrates are very important as decomposers and primary consumers. They also move through the compost, carrying smaller micro-organisms on their surface or in their gut.

Mites

Mites are eight-legged animals related to spiders and ticks. Some mites are large enough to be seen with the naked eye while others are microscopic. Mites can scavenge on leaves and other organic material, specialise in eating fungi, or are predators of nematodes, insect larvae, other mites and springtails.

Springtails

Springtails are extremely numerous in compost or under mown grassy swards. They are very small and easily identified by their habit of jumping when disturbed. They feed on decomposing plant waste, pollen, arthropod droppings and fungi.

Earthworms

Earthworm tunnelling aerates the soil and enables water and oxygen to move quickly into the soil profile. Inside the earthworm's gut, particles of organic matter are finely ground and conditioned by calcium carbonate secreted from a special gland. The digestive juices contain strong enzymes and fermenting substances. Fresh worm castings have high bacteria numbers and available nitrogen, calcium, magnesium, phosphorus and potassium. Earthworms excrete polysaccharides (sugars) that line their tunnels, preserving them for many years. They are vital in the concluding stages of composting, where they continually rework material in the maturing heap.

Slaters

Slaters or woodlice have armadillo-like armour and are related to crabs and crayfish. They are often seen in the garden, where they are sometimes mistaken for a pest. In fact they are very active decomposers. If seen on a damaged plant, they are probably eating dead plant tissues.

Slugs and snails

Slugs and snails feed on fresh plant debris and do have a useful role in the composting process.

Centipedes

Centipedes are fast-moving predators found mostly in the top few centimetres of soil and in the compost heap. They feed on small worms, insect larvae and arthropods — mainly insects and spiders. Centipedes are not particularly dangerous, although a small percentage of humans are allergic to their sting, so it makes sense to wear gloves when lifting organic matter or moving old timbers, as they like to shelter under rubbish.

Millipedes

Millipedes feed mainly on decaying plant remains. They are slower and more round than centipedes, which are flattened. Millipedes have two pairs of appendages on each body segment.

Beetles

Common soil-dwelling 'ground' beetles feed on insects, snails, slugs and other small animals. Some beetles also feed on fungal spores.

Ants

Ants move enormous quantities of mineral-bearing soil and transport soil organisms around.

Flies

Some flies pupate in the compost, and some fly larvae are parasites of soil-dwelling organisms. When they emerge from the pupae, flies transport compost organisms to new sites. Maggots will not survive high temperatures, so they can be destroyed by turning the heap and adding nitrogen-rich material. To avoid a problem with flies do not use meat or fish waste in the compost.

Earwigs

Earwigs are both predators and decomposers, feeding on decaying vegetation. Some species are specialised for hunting or grazing, but most are opportunistic consumers.

Spiders and other arachnids

Spiders feed on insects and other small invertebrates, and pseudoscorpions are fierce predators of nematodes, mites, insect larvae and earthworms.

Each category of invertebrates may contain many different species of individuals. The population may change as the heap matures, or according to the season. If you compost in the same spot repeatedly, the range and variety of insects and small animals will gradually increase. Use common sense to avoid direct contact with them, but also try to overcome irrational fears. Almost all of these small life forms are the gardener's friend, performing all manner of clean-up jobs — for free!

4. Building a compost heap

'The production of humus is the essential first step for the aspiring organic gardener.'
PETER BENNETT, *ORGANIC GARDENING*, 1986

There are many ways to make good compost. Some methods are better than others for retaining nutrients, preventing smells or managing difficult waste materials. Various methods require more space, or more careful attention to management of the heap.

Compost is not hard to make, but it does require preparation to make the most of this essential garden input. Good compost is not made in an unmanaged heap. An anaerobic heap of refuse at the end of the garden will conserve organic matter, but with minimal effort the heap could be sweet, crumbly, dark-coloured compost, full of health for your soil.

The composting site

If possible, select a level or gently sloping site. You will need access for a wheelbarrow or a trailer, and good drainage away from the heap. Some shade in summer will help to reduce water loss. If you must make the heap in the open, check the moisture content from time to time during the dry season, and add water when necessary. Exposure to the sun in winter will help the pile to heat. Be aware that the roots of some trees will try to invade the heap.

Deciduous trees such as oaks are reasonably safe. Their roots will enter the compost, but they will not grow much above the normal soil surface layer. If roots are invasive, turn the compost often, or use a weed mat or weed-stop fabric on the soil under the compost. Ideally, bury the fabric under 5cm of soil. Fine root hairs will pass through woven products, but thicker roots cannot penetrate.

Never make any compost under conifers. The chemicals contained in rainwater dripping from the needles will inhibit microbial breakdown.

You may want to consider the aesthetics of the site. If you don't maintain the composting area it can look unsightly, so you may want to keep it out of view.

It is best to keep the compost in one location for a few years, so that a good population of composting bugs can build up in the soil. Alternatively, try to build the compost on the site of a future garden bed.

If the compost gets too wet, nutrients will leach away, so cover winter heaps with layers of straw or tarpaulins to shed water. Keep compost drainage away from stormwater drains, creeks and streams, as it may contain concentrated nutrients, seeds or disease organisms.

Heap size

To create internal heat, the minimum dimension of the heap should be 1 cubic metre. A heap of at least this size will have an ideal surface area to volume ratio. The outer layers of the heap insulate the inside, so for good weed and pathogen control you should turn the heap and rebuild it carefully so that the old outer layer becomes the core of the new heap.

Larger heaps can be made, but they may create too much heat. The maximum width or height considered desirable is about 2.5m. The third dimension, length, can be as large as needed for the volume of material, giving rise to what is called a 'windrow' shape.

Very large heaps can get so hot that they smoulder from the inside, and organic matter is actually burnt up, or lost, rather than conserved. They need special attention to water levels, and should be turned if they overheat. There is a danger of spontaneous combustion in a very large heap that has been allowed to dry out.

Compost bins

In smaller gardens, bins or other methods of containing the compost are ideal. Bins look neat, and can be made rat-proof by digging them into the soil and keeping the lid on. Bins also permit better regulation of moisture content and temperature because they reduce evaporation and are easily covered during rain. Permanent compost bin structures are also the most practical system for a really productive garden. A bin system with three chambers is best.

Bins can be made of any size or shape, and from a variety of materials. The simplest is a circular container made from fencing wire and tomato stakes. A good size is 1–2m in diameter and at least 1.2m tall. Bins can also be made from wood or brick. The straw bale system (see page 35) is actually a type of bin.

Raw material for the compost is collected around the garden — for example, a pile of weeds and prunings, a bucket of ashes, kitchen waste, shredded

The Indore system

Between 1904 and 1934 the British agricultural scientist Sir Albert Howard and his colleagues studied methods of decomposing various wastes (including human sewage) that would prevent the survival of harmful organisms, or pathogens. He worked at Indore, a province of India, and his recommended way of constructing a compost heap is known as the Indore system.

The technique recommends that you start building the heap with a thick layer of carbon-containing materials, such as straw, dry leaves and old weeds. Then pile on a thinner layer of nitrogen-containing materials, such as manures and grass clippings. Next, a thin layer of soil is placed over the lot, and the sequence is repeated, adding alternate layers of carbon and nitrogen materials, plus a scattering of soil.

The original Indore system suggested using large quantities of soil as a capping over the heap, because Howard was composting human faeces. As it is not appropriate to compost human waste in Australia, except in a composting toilet, much less soil is required.

The Indore system is the easiest and most common construction method. Layers of carbonaceous and nitrogenous material are built on top of each other to construct the heap. Micro-organisms can be added by placing a sprinkling of soil between the organic layers. If weeds or manures are used there will usually be organisms present on the roots or within the waste product and additional soil is not required. Some books recommend too much soil. The organisms reproduce so quickly that few are required initially and too much soil can reduce the maximum temperature reached inside the heap. Compost organisms in ideal conditions can double their numbers every 30 minutes. Too much soil replaces vital organic matter, which is the food source for bacteria and fungi.

Types of composting bins

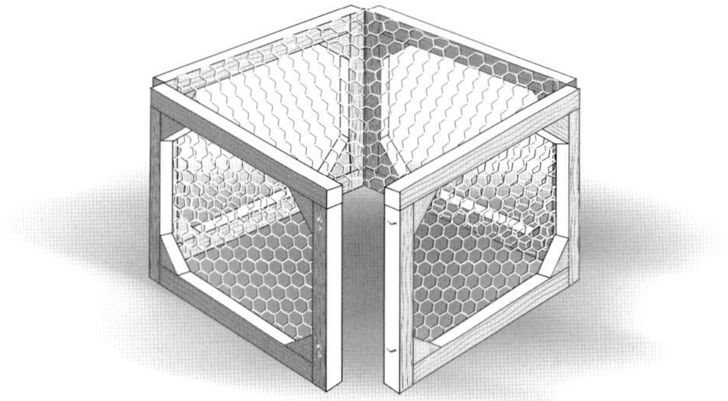

Wire and mesh bin

Wooden bin

Cement block bin

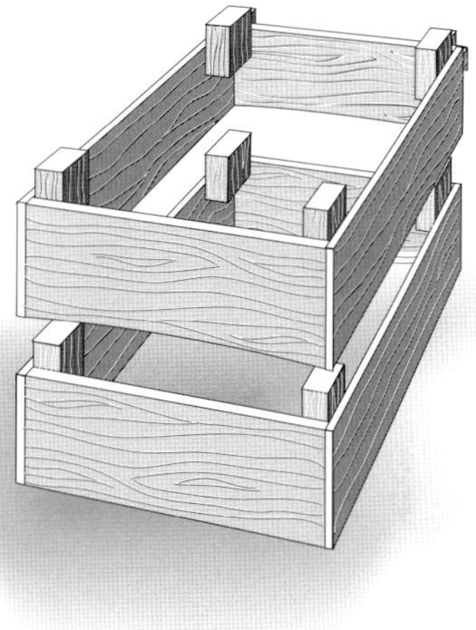

Stacking bin

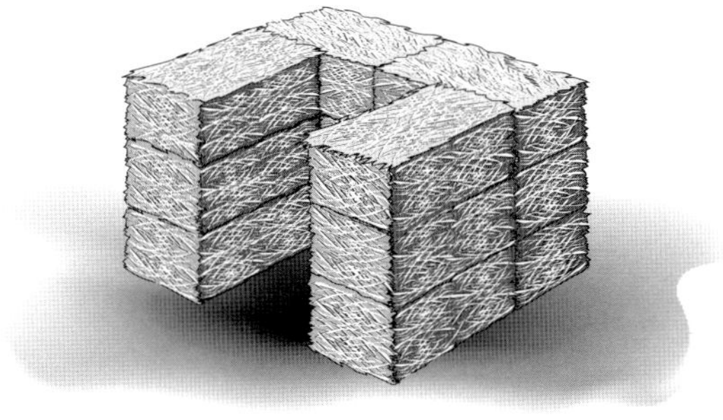

Straw bale bin

paper and manure. Bags of animal manure are readily available at garden centres or can be picked up on roadsides in the country. On the day you decide to make your compost, visit the greengrocer with sacks or boxes to collect vegetable waste.

The raw material can then be layered into the first bin and watered. If following the basic compost system described on pages 14–16, place a pole through the centre of the heap, or use one pole for every metre of windrow if making an open heap. After three to five days the compost will have started to heat and air will be excluded by the reduction in volume. At this stage, pull out the pole to get air into the heap. When the temperature starts to fall, turn the heap into the next bin. If the heap is to be turned often, it can be turned back into the first bin, then the second again, while new material is accumulated for the next compost. When the compost no longer reheats when turned, it is ready for the last bin. The last bin is for maturing compost. Start filling it from one end, and then start using the oldest compost first.

Wooden compost bins

To make a wooden compost bin, use rot-resistant timber or wood treated with an environmentally safe preservative, otherwise it will decompose after a few compost cycles. The bins should be at least 1–2m wide and 1m deep. Placing removable wooden boards at the front will make filling and turning easy. Some ingenious designs include totally demountable bins, which can be taken apart, from around the standing heap, and rebuilt facing the old heap, ready to receive the new heap as it is turned.

Factors to remember when building the heap

Good aeration

The most desirable and easily managed varieties of compost organisms need oxygen to efficiently decompose organic waste. To maintain good aeration:

- build the heap loosely
- turn the pile often, at least once per month; once per week is ideal
- do not walk on the heap.

Moisture

The right level of moisture is essential for microbial activity. If the compost pile becomes dry it will stop decomposing efficiently. Adequate moisture is reached when every particle feels damp, but free moisture cannot be squeezed from the compost. Too much moisture will fill up the air spaces between particles, excluding the oxygen and causing the process to become anaerobic. Cover the heap if there is excessive rain, or water the pile as needed to maintain decomposition.

Particle size

The smaller the size of the particles, the faster the compost organisms can work on them. Smaller particles have more surface area on which the compost organisms can work. Use a garden shredder or run over stalks with the lawn mower before putting them in the heap. If you shred woody

How long will it take?

Different conditions can cause the length of time to finished compost to vary greatly. Was the C:N ratio right? Was the material shredded? Was water adequate? Was air limited? Was the heap turned? In warm weather the process will be shorter, and a well-managed compost, turned four or five times and left, can mature in three to four months. Unshredded material and unmanaged heaps may take more than twelve months to finish. A heap that finishes in four months during summer could take up to two months longer in winter, even if managed in exactly the same way.

See also the Maye Bruce quick return method on page 58.

The long-handled compost fork is an excellent tool for moving large amounts of organic matter and turning compost heaps. The extra reach saves a lot of effort when stacking the compost. (Photo courtesy of Jeff Dale)

Autumn leaves make excellent leaf mould with a high water-holding capacity.

Autumn leaves are mainly cellulose, as the tree has been busy relocating its valuable store of nutrients before shedding its foliage. This means that leaf mould is low in nutrients, but is excellent for improving soil structure.

Liquid manure can be made and stored in these 200 litre plastic drums.

This round sieve fits perfectly over the garbage bin, creating a simple and efficient sieving system.

Worm farms are an ideal way for home gardeners to produce nutrient-rich vermicompost. (Photo courtesy of Jeff Dale)

This handful of pure worm castings was produced by a large, tropical earthworm.

This simple worm farm is made from stacked tyres. It can be seen at the Ceres Community Farm in Melbourne, where a large selection of worm farms and compost bins are on display.

This simple homemade worm farm is aerated with two pieces of plastic conduit. The large piece has holes drilled along its length, while the smaller piece is inserted into holes drilled in the sides of the barrow and through the larger pipe. There needs to be a hole in the centre of the small pipe to allow air into the larger conduit. This forms a natural convection current as air is taken in and drawn up through the larger pipe.

A biodynamic green manure crop. (Photo courtesy of Allen Gilbert)

Buckwheat can be used as a green manure crop. Its flowers are nectar-rich and attract beneficial insects to the garden. (Photo courtesy of Allen Gilbert)

wastes, or fibrous plants, or any thick, stalky material, the finished compost will be ready earlier.

Particle size may also affect the availability of vital nutrients, especially carbon and nitrogen. For example, large woodchips are a good bulking agent and help to increase aeration in the heap, but they will provide available carbon at a slower rate than the same weight of sawdust or wood shavings, and much slower than dry straw.

Carbon to nitrogen ratio

The rate of microbial activity is directly affected by the carbon to nitrogen ratio of the organic waste. Micro-organisms require a certain balance in their 'diet', including nitrogen for metabolism and growth. A shortage of nitrogen will slow down the composting process and the heap will take longer to finish. Using a lot of dry organic matter, such as autumn leaves, old dried weeds, straw and sawdust can cause a nitrogen shortage. Prevent this by using fresh, actively growing material, such as recently pulled leaves, fruit wastes and lawn clippings. Animal manures also contain nitrogen. If you have a lot of material with a high content of carbon relative to nitrogen, such as straw or sawdust, add manures, liquid seaweed or liquid compost (see the recipe on page 74).

Avoid lime

One of the most common misconceptions about aerobic compost is that you should add lime. Lime should be used when composting anaerobically in plastic bins, and worms in a worm farm require a little lime, but most open compost heaps will not benefit from lime. It is true that organic acids are produced during the initial stages of the composting process, causing a decrease in the pH. However, the pH will recover naturally in time, as the heap matures, and according to the normal changes in the balance and mix of composting organisms. A good, finished compost usually ends up slightly alkaline (pH 7.1–7.5). Adding lime to the early stages of composting causes soluble ammonium nitrogen to convert to ammonia gas, causing a loss of valuable organic nitrogen from the heap.

Manure-free compost

It is not necessary to use animal manures to make good compost. You can also make a very good 'vegetarian' compost from green material only by following these basic rules:

- three-quarters of the compost must be green, succulent growth, such as lawn clippings, freshly pulled weeds, or kitchen waste
- use a variety of different materials to ensure good nutrition, especially the presence of trace elements, and to keep the heap active
- mix dry materials thoroughly into the heap during construction, or by turning after initial heating
- the heap will need little or no watering initially because actively growing material will already have an ideal moisture content
- maintain the heap as usual.

Barrel or drum composting methods

Barrel or drum compost systems suit small gardens well and can make finished compost in a relatively short period of time. You can either purchase a compost barrel or make your own.

A homemade barrel can be made from any container of at least 200 litres capacity with a top that can be firmly secured. Ensure that the barrel has not been used to store toxic chemicals. Drill eight or ten rows of 4mm holes along the length of the barrel to facilitate air circulation and allow excess moisture to drain out. Place the barrel on its side on blocks or bricks so air can enter from the bottom. Three-quarters fill the barrel with organic matter, add a shovelful of blood and bone, and then water until the waste is moist but not soggy. Turn the drum every few days or roll it on its side to mix and aerate the compost.

This method produces very rapid compost, but it has not been through a thermophilic stage, so weed seeds may persist in the finished product. Use only clean ingredients in barrel compost — that is, ingredients that are not diseased or weedy. Clean ingredients include straw, shredded paper, weeds pulled prior to flowering and various processing wastes, for example coffee grounds.

Burying organic wastes

Some gardeners still prefer to bury organic waste directly into the soil. Most keen organic gardeners prefer composting in heaps, because it produces a fine humus product and they tend to dig their soil as little as possible. Still, the incorporation of good organic waste does compensate for the damage done to soil structure and biology by digging. Another disadvantage with this method is that you cannot plant into the soil until the wastes have decomposed — a minimum of six weeks in ideal conditions.

To bury organic wastes such as kitchen scraps, you have to dig deeper than one spade depth, or they may be dug up by cats, dogs, foxes, rats or possums. Other waste materials can be dug in to a single spade depth.

One method is to use a system of double digging, in a trench. Every few days dig a little more of the trench, digging out the first layer and stockpiling it on the soil in front, then dig the last few days' kitchen scraps into the bottom of the trench and replace the original layer on top. Next time, dig another row, until the whole bed has been turned over. Then the bed can be sown to green manure, and latter cropped with vegetables. A continuous system like this can allow a garden to be planted progressively from one side as the wastes progressively convert to nutritious compost.

Chicken composting systems

Chickens can be fed vegetable waste or grain in a pen covered with a litter of straw, seaweed, shredded paper, wood

Burying animal faeces

Domestic animal faeces should be buried deeply because they can cause disease in humans and the animals from which they came. Dig a deep hole with a posthole digger or spade, and insert a kitchen garbage bin or rubbish bin with the bottom cut out. Collect faeces from around the garden and place them into the hole and close the lid. This doggy-doo system can be left in place for several years, because some of the humus that is slowly produced in the pit will be gradually and safely incorporated underground, by earthworms. Leave the site untouched for at least two years after the last faeces are added before using it for food production.

Tim Marshall's straw bale compost system

For many years I have used straw bales to contain my compost. Gardening books often recommend wire or wooden enclosures, but straw bales have many advantages, especially if you need to turn the compost.

If the moisture and carbon to nitrogen ratios are good, turning the compost at least four to five times will produce the high temperatures necessary to kill weeds and diseases. Turning also ensures that all the contents of the pile go through the hot, interior section of the heap and allows you to view the heap to check that moisture and other factors are okay, plus reduces the time needed to finish the compost.

The bales are easily moved out of the way to allow access to the heap for turning or removing finished compost, and they can be made to any shape. The compost can also be easily moved to another site.

Straw bales fit almost any size area, except the smallest gardens. They can be made to conform to slopes, which can reduce labour if the heap is started on high ground and turned downhill. They also insulate the heap, and retain the high temperatures longer and conserve moisture better than wood or wire.

Best of all, the bales provide a perfect refuge for worms when the compost is too hot or wet, and eventually become matted with worm castings. When the bales finally start to fall apart they can be added to a new compost pile or broken into 'biscuits', which are ideal mulch.

When the bales are really old they fall apart readily. They can usually be hauled around for six months or so, and can last between 18 and 24 months under wet temperate conditions.

Wheat straw lasts longer in the bale, but pea straw adds some nitrogen. Lucerne provides the best nutritional input if you can afford it. Avoid meadow hay because it is likely to be contaminated with weed seeds. Grasses may sprout in the wheat straw, so turn the bales over occasionally to control this growth.

Arrange the bales like bricks in a wall to create bays, and turn compost between the bays, working with gravity as an aid whenever possible.

Use biscuits of straw from the bales to cover the compost in summer. Covering the heap slows water loss. To stop excessive wetting of the bay in winter, place boards across the bales and spread tarpaulins over the boards. This leaves an air space between the cover and the heap, so the compost can continue maturing during the winter months without becoming waterlogged.

shavings or sawdust. The chickens will pick out live seed, mix the green waste with straw bedding and their own droppings, and prepare the material for composting. The pen can be cleaned out occasionally and refilled with new litter. Old pen contents can be piled into a heap or bin, and will compost rapidly to a potent compost. One hen can easily produce 10kg of manure and feather waste per year.

Sheet composting

There are many definitions, or interpretations, of the practice of 'sheet composting' and many unhygienic practices occur under its guise. When an area of new soil is to be developed, it sometimes makes sense to apply large quantities of raw material directly to the soil surface and let nature take its course. This can be overdone, and some plants are smothered, killed or inhibited by lack of oxygen or by the type and concentration of plant chemicals released under sheet compost.

Sheet composting is adding a thick mulch layer to the soil, ideally with some attention to C:N ratio, so that the composting process occurs *in situ*. It combines the benefits of mulching and composting. In tropical areas, thick layers of organic material will process rapidly. In warm areas, with adequate attention to moisture, the process can also be very useful, especially for rapidly increasing organic matter and improving biological activity in new garden areas. In cooler areas, the process may not occur quickly enough, and it may be better to compost the material in a heap, and grow green manures in the new garden bed, prior to the main crop. In either situation, you will not be able to plant annual crops immediately.

Perennial plants are often less sensitive to sheet composting. Fruit trees may be able to withstand a very thick organic layer, and the process can be used in the vegetable garden between crops.

Another situation where sheet composting is useful is in developing new areas of heavy clay soil, where any form of cultivation is difficult, and potentially damaging to soil structure.

A few handfuls of earthworms collected from the compost or worm farm can be placed around the sheet mulch. The worms may not travel far from the place where you introduce them, preferring to stay close and consume all the available food in one spot, so tuck them under in several places.

Sheet composters should take extra caution to avoid including unhygienic materials in the heap, such as meat and fish wastes. Watch for slimy layers under the surface too, or 'off' smells caused by anaerobic conditions. If air can't get to the bottom of the compost layer, it won't be reaching soil and plant roots either. Grass clippings are particularly likely to become matted and stop air movement.

5. Compost ingredients

'The most logical way of preserving the richness and of enriching a farm is certainly that of applying a sufficiency of manure and vegetable matter in a decomposed state.'

James Madison (Fourth President of the United States), 1818

Most organic materials are suitable for composting. Some materials may pose a health hazard or create a nuisance and therefore should not be used to make compost. Beware of dusty materials that form a cloud when moved. Legionnaire's disease and other diseases are potentially spread in aerosols. Adding faeces requires skilled and careful composting to avoid the transmission of diseases. The use of human or pig faeces may be illegal in your area. Meat, bones, grease, whole eggs, dairy products and other putrescible wastes should not be added because they encourage disease. They may also attract rodents to the site.

Organic matter composts more quickly if bruised or chopped up into smaller pieces. This provides a larger surface area for the composting organisms to work on. Use a garden shredder or the lawn mower to chop larger material down to size.

Here are some readily available materials and how to use them:

- Grass clippings can be composted effectively, but it is advisable to mix them with other garden wastes to prevent them becoming matted or compacted and restricting airflow through the heap.
- Branches and twigs should be shredded or chipped before adding to the heap.
- Include kitchen wastes such as vegetable and fruit scraps, tea leaves, coffee grounds and eggshells.
- Sawdust from untreated wood may be added in moderate amounts. If using larger quantities, additional nitrogen must be applied.
- Wood ashes act as a source of lime and if used should only be added in small amounts. Three large shovelsful in a garden heap is enough.
- Newspaper can also be composted, but its nitrogen content is low so large amounts of paper will slow down the rate of decomposition. If paper is added to the heap it should not be more than 10 per cent of the total weight of the material in the compost pile. Shredded paper from the office is easier to use than newspaper.

Other organic materials that add nutrients to the compost pile include blood and bone, livestock manure, non-woody clippings, vegetable and flower garden refuse, hay, straw and seaweed. Livestock manure and poultry litter are ideal nitrogen sources for composting.

Compost versus manure

Is compost better than manure? After all, compost involves a lot of work so wouldn't it be easier just to use manure?

The nutrient content of manure is very variable, depending on the nature and quality of the feed, the type of bedding material and storage conditions. Nitrogen levels decline with storage, but nitrogen and potassium levels decline much more rapidly if the heap is exposed to intense rainfall. Remember that for stable manures much of the value is in urine trapped in the bedding, but this is easily leached out. If you can't compost all the material store it under cover, in a large heap with the smallest surface area, or in bags.

If you put fresh stable manure on cold soil in winter, with plants that are not actively growing and using nutrients, winter rain may leach enough nitrogen to damage tender plant roots. If you have a strongly growing, heavy feeding plant, such as a tall, staking variety tomato during the rapid growing phase, it will thrive on fresh horse or cow manure mulch. The same mulch used when the tomato has ceased rapid vegetative growth and is flowering or fruiting could damage the plant and cause flowers to fail or fruit to have poor taste, poor texture and inferior keeping quality.

If, on the other hand, shavings-based stable manure is stored in the open and subjected to strong rainfall, it will leach most of the nitrogen. If leaching happened before any significant level of composting occurred, the shavings will now cause nitrogen robbery if dug into the soil.

Manure does suit some uses, therefore, but compost is perfectly safe for any garden application.

Compost activators

Commercial compost activators are generally only necessary:

- when very rapid composting is required
- in large commercial compost heaps where they are used to encourage rapid decomposition and reduce smells
- when large quantities of sterile materials such as paper or sawdust or other difficult to manage ingredients are used
- to start a compost heap working in very low ambient temperatures (below about 8–10°C).

At other times, attention to providing a variety of ingredients, moisture and aeration, and a handful or two of soil sprinkled through the heap are adequate to start the compost working. Fresh manure is the cheapest and easiest compost activator. A shovelful of the previous compost is another simple way to activate the heap.

Activators can work in two ways. They either supply nutrients to ensure that compost organisms are not limited by lack of nitrogen or trace elements, or they add compost critters to the heap. Or they may do both.

Nutrients should not be a limiting factor if you have collected a variety of materials and if you are including high-value nutritional inputs such as kitchen waste. If you think your compost lacks nutrition, include natural activators such as lucerne, blood and bone, bonemeal, fish meal, seaweed or liquid seaweed and fresh animal manures.

'Hot' animal manures such as poultry manure and cow manure are the best activators, but horse manure works well too. The manures must be fresh to be of maximum value. If they have been dried or leached by rainfall they will be much less valuable, but still useful compost ingredients. If manure is in short supply, make a liquid 'tea' in a drum and water the heap with it. This is the best way to distribute small quantities of manure evenly through the heap. The high micro-

Comparison of compost and manure

Attribute	Compost	Manure
Nitrogen content	Variable, depending on source material	Variable, depending on feed, age and storage conditions
Nitrogen stability	Nitrogen in compost is in a stable form, so little will be lost	Manures contain readily available nitrogen, which can be lost to the atmosphere or in rain; repeated wetting and drying, and aging, will reduce the nitrogen content
Phosphorus and potassium	Readily available in finished compost	Less readily available to plants
Humus levels	High	Low
Activation of micro-organisms	Finished compost provides a home for organisms, but the activity peak has declined	Manure contains raw organic matter, which provides energy for micro-organisms
Weeds, seeds and pathogens	Thermophilic compost will not contain weed seeds or pathogens; vermi-compost and anaerobic compost may contain weeds and pathogens	Spores and seed may still be viable after passing through the animal; no heating process occurs to kill organisms
Waiting period prior to planting	Can plant immediately	May need to wait three to six weeks to avoid inhibition of germination
Soil structure effects	Excellent short- and long-term benefits	Fewer short-term benefits but contributes to medium and long-term benefit
Use on legume crops	Suitable for use	Not recommended because soluble nitrogen will suppress nitrogen fixation
Human health considerations	Suitable for use on any crops	Avoid use on leafy greens or vegetables that may be consumed raw
Personal safety considerations	Generally safe but use a face mask if dusty, or water the compost to reduce dustiness before moving	Always wear a face mask if moving large quantities, or in dusty conditions or confined spaces (e.g. chicken coop)
Cost	Moderate to high	Low to moderate

organism content of fresh manure means that it acts as an inoculum as well as a nitrogen source.

Commercial activators that contain concentrated nutrients will generally not hold these nutrients in an organic form, and will not contain nutrients that cannot be supplied just as well from organic sources.

The second type of compost activator is really an inoculum, meaning that it contains live, although possibly dormant, organisms that will decompose the organic wastes. It is possible that compost starters or activators may contain particularly vigorous and effective strains of bacteria or other organisms that are able to rapidly consume tough organic wastes, but if heaps are continuously built in the same

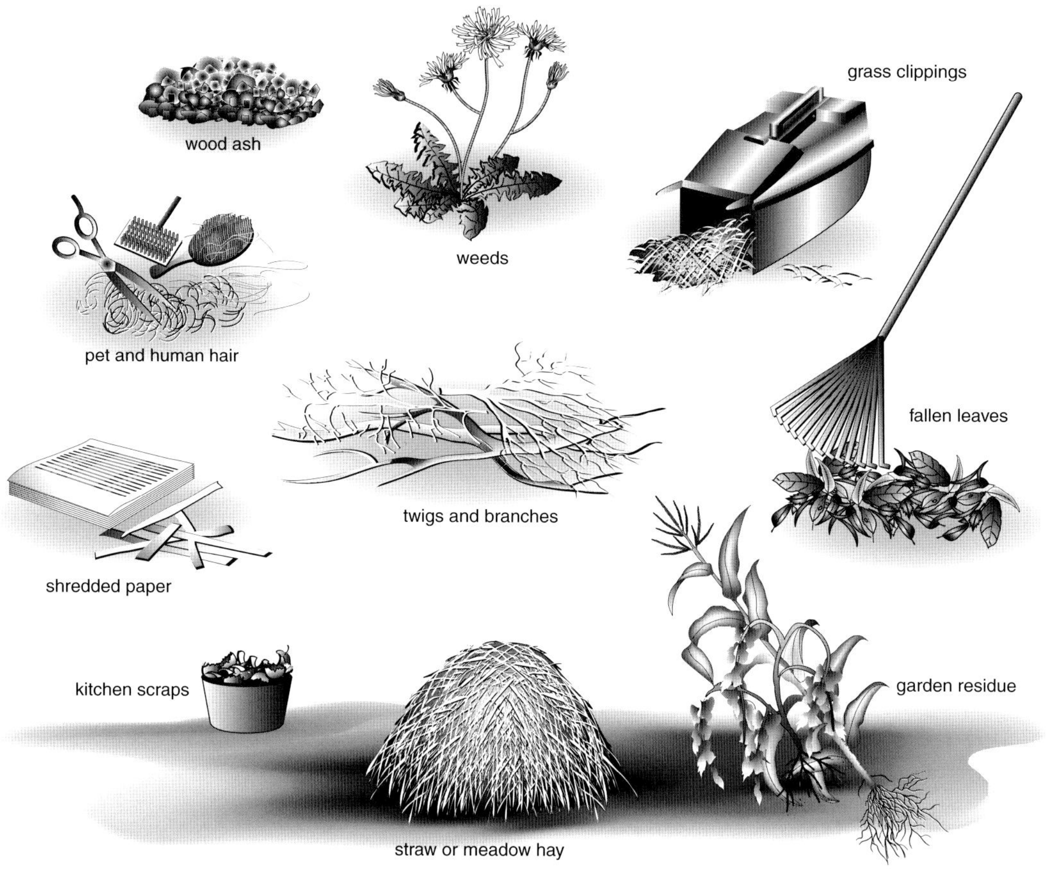

Composting materials

place, a population of naturally adapted compost bugs will soon develop. If a variety of materials are brought in, and from different sources, a wide range of composting organisms will collect under the heap, ready to inoculate the next heap. Any materials piled on the soil surface will contain soil particles. Adhering to the soil are small compost critters, and they breed so quickly that very few are needed, in the right conditions.

Sawdust and wood shavings, coal dust, rock dust and shredded paper are excellent compost materials but they are sterile, containing very few living or resting-stage decomposing organisms to break them down. Therefore, they should be:

- mixed with highly biologically active materials, such as animal manures, or
- treated with a commercial inoculum, or

> The best and most convenient compost starter is a few shovels of the last successful compost, distributed through the new heap. In this way you can think of compost as a ferment, such as yoghurt, sour dough or ginger beer. It is really the same heap continuing over time.

- mixed with enough older compost to inoculate the sterile material.

Some plant materials, such as rice hulls and wheat or oaten straw are also relatively sterile, compared to kitchen waste, lawn clippings and pulled weeds. If the compost contains a large quantity of these ingredients then it will benefit from use of an activator.

Value of different manures

Manure source	Nitrogen level	Comments
Pigeon	Hot (high)	Very good nitrogen source. Mix with high carbon materials such as paper and sawdust for C:N balance. If in short supply, make liquid tea and water the heap. The manure is so good because the birds feed on concentrated food — grains and seeds — and process their food quickly. The result is manure with a lot of nutrients, including nitrogen.
Poultry	Hot	A good source of nitrogen. Always compost pigeon and poultry manure because they are too strong to use directly on the soil. Poultry manure is ideal to mix with dry materials. Actual value of all manures will vary depending on the type and quantity of bedding material, and the age of the manure.
Cow	Cold (low)	Fresh cow manure is one of the best ingredients for compost. At least 40 per cent of fresh cow manure is made up of the dead bodies of bacteria from the bovine gut, making it an ideal compost starter. Nitrogen is lower than in poultry or horse manure.
Horse	Hot	Horses are inefficient digesters, so there is plenty of food value left in the fresh manure to start bacteria working in a new heap. Horse manure is an ideal compost ingredient.
Sheep	Cold	The hard pellets last a long time on the soil surface if used as mulch, but they disappear quickly in well-tended compost.
Pig	Warm (medium)	Pig manure is available as slurry or, more usually, dried. It is best used recomposted with other materials.
Rabbit	Warm	Depending on the rabbit's diet, this manure can contain as much, or more, nitrogen than poultry manure, but it is drier and naturally pelletised. Well suited to use through a worm farm.

Note: The actual value of all manures will vary depending on the type and quantity of bedding material, and the age of the manure.

Compost materials: source, value and how to use

Material	Comments	Source
Algae	Pond algae is a good nutrient source.	Collect from ponds and dams
Ash	Wood and paper ashes are okay to use in a compost heap. Do not overuse — two or three bucketsful in a large heap is adequate. Supplies potassium. In larger quantities wood ash may have a strongly alkalising effect, and can inhibit microbes. Beware of high sulphur and iron or other residues in coal ash. Make sure that ashes have cooled before adding to the heap.	Collect from wood fires
Bananas	Bananas and banana wastes provide phosphorus and potassium.	Collect waste from fruit processors, markets or shops
Blood and blood meal	Good nitrogen source	Available from garden centres
Blood and bone	May be directly added to compost — up to 1–2 per cent of the heap by weight.	Available from garden centres
Bonemeal	Phosphorus and nitrogen source	Available from garden centres
Bones	Best crushed prior to use. May attract vermin. May take several times through a compost heap to decompose. Soften bones by storing in wood ash, then roll and crush them on a concrete surface to make bonemeal.	Use bones from the kitchen, or collect from a butcher
Cardboard	May need to be ripped or pre-soaked if incorporated into the body of a compost heap, otherwise it produces air and water-inhibiting layers. You can use this to your advantage by building compost heaps on several layers of cardboard to limit tree-root invasion or by covering heaps with layers of cardboard and then incorporating the cardboard into a future heap, when it collapses. Several layers of thick cardboard under a heap will prevent all but the most invasive tree roots for some months.	Supermarkets and other stores
Carpet	Beware synthetic carpets, which will not break down, and old carpet may be treated with long-lasting pesticides. Use only as a compost cover, not in the compost.	Local tip
Charcoal	Small amounts of charcoal from natural wood fires are okay. If they survive composting they can be sieved out or safely used in soil or as mulch. Alternatively, soak charcoal in manure tea then bury in the garden as a 'slow-release nutrient pill'.	From wood fires
Citrus skins and pulp	Citrus waste makes excellent compost material because it contributes potassium. Mix with lawn clippings, weeds and other waste.	Collect waste from fruit processors, markets or shops

Compost materials: source, value and how to use (cont.)

Material	Comments	Source
Coffee grounds	This excellent compost ingredient contributes nitrogen. Makes good dark compost and can be used to deodorise strong-smelling materials.	Available from cafés and restaurants
Conifers	Can be composted, but are initially rot resistant. Shred and mix with other readily compostable materials.	Do not use on growing plants unless composted for several months
Cooking oil or fat	Requires a well-made heap to compost safely. Novices should avoid cooking oils or fats, except for small amounts of waste from the kitchen. Best to make a hole in the top of the heap, pour in the oil and cover with compost to stop rodents, dogs and foxes from scavenging	Kitchen waste only, do not use large quantities
Faeces	Manures from vegetarian animals are excellent compost ingredients. Manure from carnivorous domestic animals such as dogs and cats may contain harmful parasites such as tapeworm and toxoplasmosis. Best not to use.	Collect from gardens or farms
Feathers	Good nitrogen source	Home chicken coop or poultry farm
Fish waste	Fish waste must be buried deeply in a hot compost to remove risk of attracting vermin. It has high nutrient value, especially nitrogen. Also see shellfish.	Fishing enthusiasts
Grape marc	Grape marc (seed waste), skins and stalks are useful compost ingredients. The marc can contain reasonably large quantities of salt, so it should be mixed with other clean material, or watered in a heap to leach salt out.	Local wineries
Grass clippings	Contain lots of nitrogen if fresh. Mix with other materials to prevent dry, crusty or wet patches.	Own garden or mowing contractors
Grey water	Compost may be irrigated with grey water if environmentally friendly soaps and cleaning products are used. Note: Grey water is water that has been used for purposes such as washing clothes or showering. Black water (toilet water) should not be used except within an enclosed and properly designed compost toilet.	Reuse grey water from the house
Hair	Human hair and animal hair contains up to 10 per cent nitrogen, but can mat down into an air-excluding layer if used in large amounts. Mix with plenty of green waste. Avoid chemical hair dyes.	Collect from the hairdresser or barber

Compost materials: source, value and how to use (cont.)

Material	Comments	Source
Hay	Lucerne hay has most nitrogen and is a very useful compost accelerator. Pea straw has some nitrogen. Meadow hay may contain weed seeds and must be composted at a high temperature to kill any seed present. Wheat and barley straw are longer lasting (use wheat straw in bales to retain the heap). Pre-soak hay before adding to the heap.	Available from fodder stores or farms
Kitchen waste	Very good for the compost, contains a wide selection of nutrients. Use any material except meat and fish. Oyster shells etc are very good — just remove the meat to avoid scavengers. Shells will take three or four times through the heap to disintegrate. They can be crushed or used whole. Oyster shells are mainly calcium carbonate. Crushed shells are as good a calcium source as limestone.	Own kitchen or cafés and restaurants
Leaves	Leaves break down faster if green. Green leaves are an excellent general nutrient source, dry leaves contribute carbon.	Own garden
Lime and dolomite	Use as recommended directly on garden soil, but very modestly or not at all in compost. Use some lime if the heap is mainly fruit waste. Never use quicklime in compost.	Available from garden centres
Manure	Manure is a good nitrogen source. Poultry manure is the strongest. Fresh horse manure will act as a compost starter and will heat rapidly. Cow manure has a very high bacterial content. Fresh manure has the highest nitrogen content — nitrogen level diminishes with increasing age of the manure.	Available from roadside sources or farms
Molasses	It is the sugar in fresh horse manure that helps to accelerate the compost process. You can achieve the same purpose with 500g of molasses mixed with 10 litres of warm water and poured over slow composting material such as straw. This causes rapid temperature increase.	Supermarket, fodder store or health food store
Mushroom compost	Mushroom compost contains some value and will reheat if mixed with other materials. Makes very dark-coloured compost. Mushroom compost itself may contain some ingredients not considered organic, so it should be composted prior to use.	Local supplier
Newspaper	Shredded or scrunched up sheets of newspaper are okay. Large quantities of paper will mat and limit air and moisture movement in the heap. Mix newspaper with green waste and a nitrogen source. Pre-soak paper in a bucket or tub to improve wetting ability.	Reuse household newspapers
Paper	Shredded paper works best. Do not use waxed or glossy paper.	Available from local businesses

Compost materials: source, value and how to use (cont.)

Material	Comments	Source
Pine needles	Break down slowly. Do not use for more than about 15 per cent of the heap for best results.	Collect from pine forest
Rock dust	Crushed basalt and other materials can be used to enrich the mineral content of compost. Maximum 2.5 per cent of the heap.	Available from garden centres
Rock phosphate	Pulverised rock phosphate can be added to compost to the maximum 1 to 2 per cent of the heap.	Available from organic fertiliser suppliers
Sawdust	Needs to be balanced with adequate nitrogen, usually in the form of poultry or other manures. Weathered sawdust decomposes much faster than fresh. Contributes carbon.	From local wood-working businesses or mills
Sewage sludge	Sewage sludge contains important plant nutrients. The disadvantage is it may have heavy metals or other residues that preclude its use in certified organic farming. Use with care and limit the quantity applied to any one garden plot over time. Most suitable for non-food crops.	Sewage works and fertiliser suppliers
Shellfish	Prawn, lobster and crayfish shells are composed of chitin, which makes an extremely powerful plant nutrient and plays a role in disease protection. Good source of nitrogen, phosphorus and calcium. Bury deeply in the heap.	Fish processors and restaurants
Soil	Large amounts of soil are not necessary for the composting process. Small amounts may be sprinkled through the heap to introduce soil organisms. If weeds are pulled, or materials like manure are stored on soil and scraped with a shovel, sufficient soil will be introduced. When using large amounts of sterile material such as shredded paper or sawdust, add a handful of soil for every five or six shovelsful of sawdust.	Own garden
Straw	Contributes carbon and bulky organic material. May need to be pre-soaked as straw sheds moisture, and requires several irrigations to wet thoroughly.	Available from fodder stores
Tea leaves	Supply nitrogen, phosphorus and potassium.	Own kitchen or cafés
Urine	Urine contains about two-thirds of the nitrogen excreted from the body, and most of the potassium. Because these elements are in solution, they become available to plants much more quickly than those in dung. Dilute with three times the quantity of water and pour over the heap from a watering can.	Collect own urine in a flask, or capture animal urine in bedding
Weeds	Excellent compost material, especially if used fresh. Beware strong growing weeds which sprout from stolons or underground parts. Keep the heap very hot to kill them.	Own garden

Compost materials: source, value and how to use

The table on the preceding pages provides basic information on the value of different compost ingredients, how they may be used and where to source them. Although anything that lived or is the product of something that lived can be composted, some materials are much easier to find and use in a home garden compost. Keen organic gardeners try to conserve all available organic matter, and composters soon learn how each material behaves.

What to avoid

Following are some items that should not be added to a compost heap.

- Do not put plastic, aluminium foil, painted materials, foam or large amounts of grease into a compost heap. Avoid synthetic materials of any kind.
- Don't empty the vacuum cleaner into the heap because it may contain synthetic carpet fibres, plastic and chemical residues. Only use things that have lived — the exception is a small quantity of mineral rocks, up to a maximum of 2.5 per cent of the heap.
- Any plants that have been recently killed or sprayed with a herbicide, or treated with a pesticide (insecticide, weedicide, fungicide and so on) should not be composted. Diseased plants and weed seeds should not be used unless the temperature of the heap will reach 65°C or higher, for at least 48 hours.
- Large quantities of cooking oil or fatty wastes require careful attention to compost rapidly, and may attract vermin. Small kitchen quantities can be used if buried deep in the home heap.
- Meat and fish will attract flies and vermin and cause the heap to smell, so avoid putting meat residues into a home compost or vermiculture system.
- Bread and cakes attract mice so use them only in small quantities, in the centre of the heap. Crumble bread prior to adding, so that no large pieces remain in the heap.
- Pet waste and human manures can contain pathogenic parasites and require constant high temperature composting to be safe. They are not suitable for normal backyard composting, but can be used in special compost toilets.
- Sawdust from treated timber contains poisons that may kill compost organisms and could persist in the final product. Do not use treated wood sawdust or shavings.
- Composting does not kill some pernicious weeds, such as oxalis (or soursob), nutgrass, kikuyu, tradescantia and onion weed, unless very high temperatures can be maintained for a long time. They can be fermented in water for five or six weeks prior to composting or the bulbs can be crushed before adding to the heap. Other plants that will require chipping prior to composting to ensure that they are killed include common ivy, cypress, oleander, castor oil plant and hemlock.

Do not add thick layers of any one kind of material to the heap. Pre-mix the material or use shallow layers only. Also, do not add small quantities of material each day. Save them and construct the heap all at once, or over a few days.

6. Compost tools

'Composting is a way of turning a liability into an asset on the farm.'
RICHARD THOMPSON, *TOOLS FOR HOMESTEADS, GARDENS AND SMALL-SCALE FARMS*, 1978

Everyone has a favourite tool for each job. Some common garden tools are adaptable to composting uses, but good, specialised equipment makes composting easier on the body, especially when turning the heap. Most of the tools described here are available from garden centres or hardware stores. Remember that compost may have a different texture, depending on the raw materials used and the way it is made, so a tool that works perfectly in one situation may not work well in another.

Shredders

It is not necessary to shred most organic material for composting. However, shredding will speed up the decomposition process and make the heap hotter, earlier.

Use care when shredding. Avoid putting stones and soil in the shredder because they damage blades and the stones may become projectiles. Forcing too much material through will block the shredder. Feed alternate lots of woody and softer material slowly, and without too much force.

There are several options, depending on your needs.

Rotary mowers

A rotary lawn mower can be used to shred leaves, weeds and small, woody prunings. Spread the material out on a path or reasonably firm patch of soil and run the mower over until shredded.

Electric shredders

Electric shredders are suitable for small branches and prunings (up to 20mm). Some larger commercial units can handle bigger stalks. Shredders can be purchased or hired for specific jobs. Make sure the shredder is fitted with a circuit breaker.

Petrol-driven shredders

Petrol shredders are generally more powerful than electric shredders and can shred larger stalks and prunings. They can be expensive to purchase or hire, and are most suitable for gardening businesses and small farms. Larger shredders for commercial use, such as those used by tree fellers and council gardening staff, are also available.

Compost-handling equipment

Pick-up boards

Pick-up boards are an excellent tool for picking up loose, lightweight material from the ground that escapes the grip of any other tool. The boards can be made from any scrap materials — reasonably durable laminated timber, or hardboard sheets are best. They are easily made from offcuts — 450 by 300mm is ideal. If they are this long, they neatly sit across the handles of the barrow, and are always available when collecting compost materials. Just grip the boards in the middle to scoop up leaves, then release them into the barrow or onto a tarpaulin, or directly onto the compost heap.

Plastic hands

Plastic hands are available in garden centres. They are moulded plastic versions of the pick-up boards. Plastic hands undoubtedly cost more than the simple wooden boards, but they have handgrips, which makes them a little easier to control. Most designs don't pick up as much material as the pick-up boards.

Tarpaulin or garden bags

A simple tarpaulin is useful for moving loose materials such as autumn leaves. Spread the tarpaulin out, pile the leaves into the centre, gather the four corners and haul the load off to the trailer, or directly to the compost. The tarp can be pulled along concrete, bitumen or gravel paths with little damage, and it is possible to move much more loose material such as autumn leaves this way than with a wheelbarrow. The commercial version of the tarpaulin is a garden bag. They are very useful if they come with strong rope handles.

Old tarpaulins can also be used to cover the heap in winter, to shed excess rain. Place timbers over or against the sides of the heap and spread the tarpaulin over the timber, leaving an air gap between the tarpaulin and the heap to allow air to move into the heap.

Sides for the garden barrow

A good garden barrow is a necessity for keen composters. Some ingenious gardeners design extension sides for moving bulky materials around. A strong, professional-use wheelbarrow is an expensive item, but smaller garden barrows and plastic garden carts are readily available and less costly.

Some gardeners believe that a 'builder's barrow' is too big for garden use, but they are strongly made and will not twist and distort under a heavy load. They generally have very strong tyres and axles, and firm handgrips. Garden barrows are often weaker than they should be and wobble or twist when required to carry a heavy burden. This forces the driver to counterbalance the load, which can cause much more strain and injury. For serious composters, the extra cost of a builder's barrow may well be worthwhile.

Tined tools

Compost fork

A compost fork is a useful composting tool, capable of greatly reducing the effort required to turn the heap. A compost fork has four tines, not three like a pitchfork, so it can lift a large load and keep it stable. Compost forks are available with a long handle or a short handle, and both have a useful function. The short-handled tool permits good control of a large load. When using this tool, keep a safe distance away from other people, and do not overload it with heavy material. The best use for the fork is very bulky and fibrous material, such as piled weeds, grasses and straw.

The tines on a compost fork are narrow, rounded and quite pointy. They are totally unsuited to digging and the compost fork must never be used to dig into the soil because it will bend or break. It is designed only for moving loose materials above the soil surface.

The short-handled tool is better in confined spaces; the long-handled tool is better for tossing a load onto a trailer.

Pitchfork

A pitchfork has three tines and a very long handle, which makes it a dangerous tool to use if there are other people around.

Particles and spores from dry compost and materials can be a health hazard. A dust mask protects the compost-maker.
(Photo courtesy of Jeff Dale)

Investigating a biodynamic compost heap to test for maturity.

These compost bins are made from pallets lined with shadecloth.

These farm-scale compost windrows are on certified organic tea plantations in Sri Lanka.

Leaf mould is quite different from compost. It is very dark in colour, and exceptionally light and fluffy. Small pieces of leaf may still be visible, but if rubbed, they crumble into a fine powder.

This leaf mould heap is built under an oak tree. A weed matting base prevents the roots from invading.

Using pick-up boards gets the job done twice as fast. (Photo courtesy of Jeff Dale)

The biodynamic compost preparation known as '500' is a highly concentrated, specialist compost.

A large compost sieve can be made using an old wire bed base.

A large aluminium shovel is an ideal tool for the serious composter. They are lightweight, and hold a lot of bulky material.

The pitchfork was made for tossing hay up onto a cart. Less material can be moved at one time than with the compost fork, and with less stability. Use a pitchfork with care if it is the only available tool.

Garden fork

An ordinary garden fork can be used to make or turn compost. It is not very efficient because the tines are square in profile, making the fork difficult to push into a heap of material. The angle at which the tines are attached to the handle is also different. It is set for easy entry into the soil when digging, whereas the compost fork is designed for lifting and carrying a load. Use the garden fork for compost if you do not have a specialised tool — at least it has the advantage of serving several functions.

Shovels

Aluminium shovel

Broad-mouthed aluminium shovels are very useful for moving dry and light ingredients, especially if they are small enough to fall through the tines of a compost fork. The aluminium shovel can take a much bigger bite than any other tool. The short-handled version gives better control. The shovel is light, and a lot more bulky, fine-textured material, such as sawdust, can be moved with an aluminium shovel than with an ordinary garden shovel.

This tool is not designed to withstand digging, however, and is only meant for moving loose materials piled on the soil surface.

Wide-mouth shovel

A wide-mouth shovel is a common garden tool adaptable to making compost. The wide mouth holds a lot of material. The back of the shovel is flat, which allows it to be placed on the ground and pushed under a load of manure or other material. Shovels are available in long- and short-handled versions. A long handle is best for tossing a load onto a vehicle and a shorter one is best for turning the heap in a confined space. A pointy-nosed shovel is useful for digging into a more solid heap of material, such as manures that have been sitting and compacting for a long time. The wide mouth is built to move loose materials, and the pointy nose for applications that involve more digging.

Other tools

Compost turner

A compost turner is a bar with two short articulated wings at one end and a T-grip handle with plastic grips for a good purchase. The turner is thrust into the compost heap, forcing the two wings to flick back against the bar. It is then pulled back, which flicks the wings out, locking them at a 90° angle to the bar. It is then repeatedly pushed in, out and around at different points in the heap as necessary, to aerate and mix the ingredients.

A compost turner does not save labour compared to turning the heap with a fork and shovel — both involve considerable effort. The advantage of the turner is for aerating boxes in confined spaces, where the compost cannot be turned, or for compost stored in bins.

Short bursts of using the turner are easier than using it for a long time. Don't try to do the whole heap at once. Start at one end and work down a little each time you visit the heap.

Rakes

Rakes are another common garden tool adaptable to composting use. There are several basic designs, including solid garden rakes, and plastic or metal leaf rakes. The solid garden rake was designed for levelling soil. It is quite strong and can drag a large load of weeds or leaves. Whenever possible, build your compost heap on a slight incline or slope. Instead of turning the heap, remove the sides of the bin or the straw bales used to retain the heap on the downhill side, and use the rake or a hoe to pull the heap down. With gravity working for you, the job is completed more quickly and with less effort.

Metal or plastic leaf rakes are excellent tools for collecting autumn leaves, or removing gum leaves from the lawn or path. Rake the leaves, bark and other material into a heap and pick it up with the boards described on page 47, or simply rake the material directly onto a tarpaulin and drag it off to the compost heap. Alternatively, use two leaf rakes as pick-up boards.

Composting in a glasshouse

Compost can be made in a glasshouse or poly tunnel. Composting in a glasshouse in winter will help to obtain desirable temperatures within a compost heap. The heat from the compost benefits plants grown in the house, and so does a higher level of carbon dioxide. Carbon dioxide is continually released from the heap during decomposition by respiration of compost organisms.

Crowbar

A crowbar can be used to check the progress of the compost heap. Thrust it into the middle of a recently built heap and leave it there for several hours. If the compost is working well, the bar will be too hot to grip tightly when it is pulled out of the heap. A small cloud of steam should also be evident rising up from the hole when the bar is removed. If you are using a static heap (one that is not turned), use the crowbar or a tomato stake to poke airholes into the centre to aerate the material.

7. Making specific purpose composts

'Turn the clod
And wheel thy compost home.'
William Cowper

Once the compost builder has mastered the basic technique, it is possible to build a variety of different, specific purpose composts. These may include compost designed to provide a range of nutrients that are required in the garden, composts for disease control, and making leaf mould.

Leaf mould

Leaf mould is easily made. It is a very useful product that provides a soft and rich earthy material with a very high water-holding capacity. It is a most effective ingredient in potting media or where high moisture retention is needed, such as in ferneries and bog gardens. Leaf mould is suitable as a replacement for materials with high environmental cost, such as peat or sphagnum moss.

Have you seen the black powdery soil that develops under leaf mulch in the forest or in a park in places where leaves accumulate, such as under the garden bench? A good leaf mould has the same dark and soft, powdery appearance, in contrast with the crumbly soil-like product found in the regular compost heap.

Most books with instructions for making leaf mould are written for the Northern Hemisphere, and they assume that only deciduous leaves will be used. While a deciduous-leaf mould is an excellent product it is possible to build a similar product using leaves from indigenous Australian trees, including eucalypts and acacias. The finest product is made by using not more than 25 per cent eucalyptus or other leaves with a high oil content. If you have leaves only from natives, try the system described below. It may take a little longer, or produce an end product with a little less of the soft, loose feel and earthy smell characteristic of leaf mould, but it will still have the same qualities and uses.

Constructing the heap

The simplest leaf mould will be the easiest compost you ever make. Place some tomato stakes in the ground and stretch chicken wire or other material around the stakes to form a container or bin. You can retain the lower 40–50cm of the pile with corrugated iron or timber to stop gradual outflow of decomposed leaves, but this is not essential. Using a non-permeable material for the full height is not a good idea, because the heap needs oxygen to work well.

Water the soil before you start building the heap. Now place leaves in the bin, and build the heap in layers. It is best completed within about eight weeks. The time taken to construct the heap can be longer than is ideal for ordinary compost because the entire process occurs more slowly so the heap does not reach the same high temperature.

Pick-up boards are the most helpful tool for collecting leaves (see page 47). Rake the leaves into heaps and use the boards to gather them up and place in a barrow or directly into the heap. You will be surprised at the large amount of material you can move quickly in this way.

Another useful technique is to make a 'leaf-sled' from a simple tarpaulin or ground sheet. The sled works better than a barrow, which will not hold many leaves unless it has extended sides.

Pick up the leaves after a light shower. When leaves are wet they stick together, making them easier to move with a rake or compost fork. It also saves having to water the heap.

Make the heap under the shelter of trees to prevent excess drying out. You may have to experiment with the position as some trees will invade the heap with feeder roots. If this is a problem, use a barrier such as a weed mat or shadecloth. Do not make any compost under conifers because the chemicals carried by rainwater dripping from the needles will inhibit microbial breakdown. If the heap is built in the open, check the moisture content from time to time during the dry season and add water when necessary.

It is acceptable to stand on a leaf mould heap to compress it when first made. This is never recommended for a normal compost heap, which must be well aerated at all times. A leaf mould heap does not need to be turned. The leaves are spongy when fresh and will recover from some compression. They will also lose much of their volume during the process, so a very large heap can be made at first. Do not stand on or compress the heap later in the composting process.

Deciduous leaves

The deciduous tree deliberately drops its leaves. In the process leading up to leaf fall, many of the nutrients are translocated or moved to other parts of the plant. The plant stores these recovered nutrients in other tissues until they are needed for next season's growth. This means that the deciduous leaf mould is not high in nutrients. Autumn leaves are mainly composed of cellulose, which is slow and difficult to break down. The process does form very long-lasting humus, with the high water-holding capacity for which leaf mould is renowned.

Non-deciduous leaves

The same general rules apply to non-deciduous leaves that have fallen naturally. Eucalypts drop leaves throughout the year, and some nutrient stripping does occur. Leaves gathered from tree or shrub pruning will contain more nitrogen and other nutrients, and this type of leaf mould may heat up, like normal compost. In fact, leaves harvested while still growing are the richest plant-based source of minerals because they come from living plants themselves.

Additional material

Any compost materials can be put into the heap, including weeds, grass clippings, vegetable waste from the kitchen, wood ash or other organic matter. If the leaf mould is to be used as normal compost, use as many other materials as you wish. To preserve the special nature of the leaf mould, only use other materials for 20–25 per cent of the volume of the heap.

The end product

Prime leaf mould takes about two years to make, without any turning or extra nitrogen and with only an occasional sprinkling of water. A similar result can be achieved in about half the time by shredding the leaves with a nitrogen source, such as poultry manure, and by careful attention to watering. If you don't have a shredder, spread the leaves out in a courtyard or on the lawn and run over them with the lawn mower. Turning the heap over may also help to speed up the process.

In the winter in wet regions, cover the heap with a sheet of black plastic to help warm the decaying leaves and shed excess water. And if you have chickens, use the leaves as bedding for them before using them in the heap.

Store finished leaf mould in the original heap, or in a large plastic garbage bin. If you run out of mould before the next heap is finished you can take a little from the developing mould. Take some of the heap and pass it through a sieve. Some of the fine black powder will already be forming and the sieved material can be used to pot up ferns or other plants with high moisture-retention requirements.

Good topsoil can hold 60 per cent of its own weight in water. Leaf mould will hold up to 500 per cent of its weight in water. Because leaf mould retains water so well, it makes an ideal conditioning agent when scratched lightly into seedbed soil. It also makes an excellent dark, and therefore quickly warming and water-retaining, mulch for seedbeds in spring.

It is best to dig only decomposed leaves directly into the soil, unless there is plenty of time for them to fully decompose before the ground will be planted. Undecomposed leaves may release allelopathic or plant growth-inhibiting compounds during the decaying process.

Nutritional composts

It is possible to make specific nutritional compost for particular uses. For instance, bracken fronds make potassium-rich compost ideal for use on flowering orchids.

Bracken

Bracken is known as a potassium accumulator. One of the adaptations that makes bracken such an aggressive invader of grassland or woodland is its ability to scavenge potassium. This helps to establish the ecological advantage bracken has over other plants. Bracken commandeers most of the potassium, as soon as it

Quick guide to leaf mould

Use any leaves, but deciduous leaves are best for a traditional leaf mould. For the best product use less than 25 per cent eucalyptus leaves.
Build the heap in a sheltered position, such as under a deciduous tree.
Start with wet soil under the heap. Speed up the process by:

- shredding the leaves
- adding limited amounts of nitrogen
- keeping the pile moist
- turn the pile occasionally.

Leaf mould makes an ideal mulch cover for germinating seeds. Use it around ferns, in potting soil and where rapid increase in organic matter and water retention is required.

becomes available in the soil. Potassium levels are highest in the ferns midway through the growing season, when it can reach levels as high as 2.8 per cent dry weight. Late in the season, the potassium moves to the roots and rhizomes.

To make bracken compost, cut the green stems and use bracken for at least 40 per cent of the weight of ingredients, up to a maximum of 50 per cent. Mix the bracken with a nitrogen source such as fresh poultry or pigeon manure and any other ingredients to hand. Shred tough stalks to hasten decomposition.

Dandelion

Dandelion is known to be an iron accumulator, in the same way that bracken accumulates potassium. It can be collected to form an iron-rich compost.

Kelp

The kelp family of seaweeds are used to make trace-element-rich liquid manures and composts. Kelp powder is a very concentrated product. The powder or fresh kelp can be added to the heap to create a tonic compost for young or sick plants, and to improve general trace element nutrition of soils.

Herbal compost additives

Some organic and biodynamic gardeners grow herbs such as stinging nettle, comfrey, yarrow, chamomile and valerian specifically for making liquid fertiliser or for adding to the compost. These plants are rapid growing with strong underground parts, so they produce a lot of biomass and regrow readily from cuttings. They can be made to specific biodynamic preparation (see page 59), or simply plucked and added to the heap. To make better use of a small quantity, bruise the leaves and stems and soak in water for eight to 24 hours. Add water and vegetation to the compost. The rich exudate produced by their roots is full of sugars that encourage soil organisms to live in the soil. This soil can be used as a compost starter or inoculant.

Stinging nettle produces rich, green, succulent growth early in its life cycle. Because it produces so much lush growth, nettle is used for extraction of natural plant chlorophyll. At this leafy stage it produces a nitrogen-rich liquid manure or compost. When it grows and matures it collects the trace elements phosphorus and potassium. In its mature phase, stinging nettle is known to be a good phosphorus accumulator.

Comfrey recipe

Comfrey is renowned as an excellent ingredient in liquid manure (see page 75). There are many other compost recipes in organic gardening folklore and history. The Henry Doubleday Society, under the guidance of the famous organic horticulturist Lawrence D. Hills, unearthed a vast number of comfrey recipes. Here is a simple recipe for comfrey compost:

- Place alternate layers of leaf mould and freshly shredded or layered comfrey leaves in a barrel or rubbish bin.
- Use the compost when the comfrey leaves look grey, shrivelled and fall apart when touched.
- The compost provides very readily available nutrients for young seedlings.

Animal products

Hoof and horn meal or dried blood, or blood and bone meal can be added to compost to improve the nitrogen content. Hoof and horn meal can contain as much as 15 per cent nitrogen. It is available from abattoirs, steamed and redried.

Rock dust and rock phosphate

A variety of other crushed rocks or rock flours can also be added to the heap. Natural rock phosphate is more rapidly available if passed through a biologically active compost heap before applying to soil. Add rock dust and rock phosphate for a compost high in minerals and phosphorus.

Disease-fighting compost

Because compost contains many plant nutrients in a readily available form, it provides rapid first aid for struggling plants. Often nutrients like zinc may be at low levels in the soil, in an unavailable form. Zinc plays a major role in health maintenance and disease protection in plants and animals. Liquid manure made from compost can be used as a foliar spray, to help speed up the effect of trace elements.

Compost is also a biological inoculant and therefore adds many live (dormant or active) micro-organisms. Some of these make antibiotics such as penicillin and some are strongly competitive with, or antagonistic to, disease organisms.

Many organic growers use compost sprays as a general disease preventative, especially to prevent damping off of seedlings, or against bacterial spot and rust on roses. Compost is also known to be protective against *Phytophthora cinnamomi*, a soil-borne fungus that kills many native plants, as well as crops such as chestnut and avocado. Combined with sound hygiene and good organic soil management, including attention to drainage and focus on phosphorus, calcium, zinc and boron nutrition, compost has helped to save the avocado industry in Queensland and northern New South Wales.

In particular, composted tree barks have been found to play a role in disease suppression. In Germany and Europe, tree barks have been used against serious tree disease such as *Phytophthora* or Dutch elm disease. In Australia, composted bark of *Eucalyptus diversicolor* (karri) and *E. calophylla* have been found to be particularly suppressive of *Phytophthora*. Availability of these barks is limited, however, and extensive research has yet to be conducted in this area of compost science, but there is reason to suspect that other tree barks will also be found to make composts that are able to suppress disease organisms.

Before applying compost sprays to foliage for disease protection, use intense

Comfrey juice concentrate

Here is a powerful plant tonic:

- Punch a hole in the bottom of a large rubbish bin or plastic barrel and fill with comfrey leaves.
- Stand the barrel on blocks and place a small container under the hole.
- Eventually a thick, green liquid will seep out.
- Remove each day's production and store the liquid in an open bucket in a shady position. Do not store in a jar because the liquid may ferment and explode.
- Dilute with water to the colour of weak tea and use as a plant tonic or house plant fertiliser.

Sources of plant nutrients

Nutrient	Source	Comments
Nitrogen	Animal manure**, hoof and horn manure**, lucerne hay***, stinging nettle***, blood and bone*, coffee grounds, feathers, fish waste***, fresh lawn clippings*, hair, legumes such as clovers**, comfrey***, urine*, organic potassium fertilisers	Use source materials in compost or as mulch; aerobic compost retains more nitrogen than anaerobic compost (using same starting materials)
Phosphorus	Rock phosphate**, blood and bone*, bonemeal***, hoof and horn manure***, lawn clippings*, fresh green leaves*, eggshells, animal manure*, organic potassium fertilisers**	Use rock phosphates to make up 2–4 per cent of the heap to make a high-phosphate compost
Potassium	Blood and bone*, bracken**, fish waste**, leaves, animal manure*, wood ashes, fine granite dust*, certified organic potassium fertilisers*** (Langbeinite, sold as K-Mag)	Purchase certified organic fertilisers from garden centres or by mail order; refer to Yellow Pages or seek information on local resources from local and State organic gardening clubs
Calcium	Bone*, ground limestone*, seashells (oyster shells) *, wood ashes, gypsum	If using lime, use agricultural limestone only; too many wood ashes will cause loss of nitrogen, and may form layers that limit air and water movement (maximum four or five buckets in a 3 cubic metre compost heap)
Sulphur	Elemental sulphur, fresh green organic matter***, cabbage leaves***	To correct a sulphur deficiency, purchase sulphur, sometimes called 'flowers of sulphur', from a garden centre or mineral supplier; use as maximum 0.5 per cent of original heap
Magnesium	Finely ground dolomite or mica*, Epsom salts, fresh green leaves and weeds***, lawn clippings**	To correct a magnesium deficiency, dissolve Epsom salts in a watering can and sprinkle the compost heap as it is constructed
Trace elements (general)	Kitchen waste***, fresh green leaves**, seaweed (including fresh, liquid and powdered forms) **, weeds**, wood ashes	Use a variety of materials to ensure best spread of trace elements
Iron	Dandelion***, stinging nettle***, silver beet**, seaweed**, iron chelate	Use as leaf spray

**** preferred source **ideal source *next choice*

agitation, including shaking or stirring, to bring beneficial organisms into the suspension.

Biodynamic compost

Biodynamics is a specialised form of organic growing developed by the Austrian philosopher Rudolf Steiner in the 1920s. Others interested in this field have since developed the biodynamic method, such as Ehrenfried Pfeiffer in America, and Alex Podolinski in Australia.

Biodynamics uses the basic organic approach, places high value on internal organisation and self-sufficiency, and uses preparations or recipes designed to capture the influence of various 'cosmic forces'. These forces can be understood as the natural rhythms of life, such as cycles of daily and seasonal changes, or they can be viewed as more 'supernatural' forces. Some practitioners believe the recipes are simply a routine incorporating a mixture of sound horticultural practice and traditional folk wisdom, others believe the right attitude and mind set are critical for success. Whatever the approach, there are many excellent biodynamic farms and gardens based on the method developed by Steiner.

The main biodynamic growing input is BD500, or horn manure. BD500 is made by burying fresh cow manure in cow horns, in fertile soil, for six months over winter.

BD501 is a silica spray, made from very finely ground silicate minerals such as felspar. It is used for enhancing the flavour of food crops and improving keeping qualities, and may have a role in disease prevention and control.

The biodynamic compost preparations are numbered 502 to 507. The manufacture of biodynamic compost preparations is complex, so the best way to obtain them is to join a local biodynamic group. Local groups usually make their preparations as part of their regular activity, and all members can participate. The process is very precise, and the depth of burying and nature or quality of materials used and storage practices are said to make a large difference. The basic recipe appears below.

The biodynamic compost preparations are added to the heap by poking holes with a stick, to about 500mm deep, between 0.5 and 2m apart. About 1g of the preparations are then separately and individually added to an average-sized heap. One preparation is poured or mixed into the bottom of each hole. The hole is then sealed with a little wet dung and closed over.

Because the biodynamic compost preparations work to enhance the breakdown of organic matter and the subsequent build-up of humus, they can be added to any form of compost heap, including open heaps, bins, leaf mould, compost toilets, worm farms, liquid compost or manure, and septic tanks.

Maria Thun's cow pat pit

Maria Thun is a biodynamic gardener and educator. Her cow pat preparation is designed to supplement rather than replace horn manure (BD500). The preparation is used during all ploughing operations, including turning in green manure and on pastures after mowing or grazing. Cow pat preparations are usually made in a wooden container, such as a wine barrel with the base removed and sunk into the ground, or a bottomless box. A lid is required. The following is a simple cow pat recipe:

- Finely grind 150g of eggshells.
- Mix the eggshells with 50 litres (or five buckets) of fresh cow manure and 500g of rock dust (basalt).
- Stir the mixture continuously for one hour.
- Transfer half the mixture to a bottomless barrel, buried into the ground, add the individual biodynamic compost preparations and then top the barrel up with the rest of the mixture.
- Add the valerian liquid (BD507) to the top.
- Seal the barrel with a lid and leave for four weeks.
- Open the barrel and stir thoroughly, then close again and leave for two weeks.
- Add 50g to 10 litres warm water, stir for 20 minutes (sufficient for one-fifth of a hectare).
- Maria suggested applying the mixture three times, on three consecutive days. Use all the mixture within three days.

Barrel compost

A variation of the cow pat pit known as barrel compost, or manure concentrate, is made by biodynamic groups. The same method is used as for Maria Thun's recipe, except that three sets of the 2g compost preparations are used. It is recommended that home gardeners activate the Barrel Compost by stirring in 5 litres of lukewarm water for 20 minutes. Use the biodynamic method of stirring. Uses for barrel compost include:

- when making a compost heap over a period of time rather than all at once, sprinkle the barrel compost over the heap or bin after each addition of new material
- add to small compost bins, tumblers, waste eliminators and so on
- sprinkle (as per BD500) over gardens, lawns (after mowing), on freshly dug-in green manure and after cultivation
- flush down the septic or compost toilet to keep it working well
- add to small batches of liquid manure.

Cow pat pit can be used whenever organic matter is added or when the soil is stimulated because it spreads the influence of the compost preparations 502 to 507 over the area, to stimulate the breakdown of organic matter and the build-up of humus.

The Maye Bruce quick return method

Maye Bruce of Cirencester, England, devised this quick return method, recommended for rapid open bin composting with no turning. The system is therefore very suited to small gardens or anyone who finds turning the heap physically challenging.

To make Maye Bruce quick return compost, follow these simple steps:

- Use a walled enclosure or bin to retain heat.
- Start the heap on a 7.5cm deep bed of rubble and charcoal. (Make your own charcoal by dowsing half-burnt wood with water.) She also suggested spraying the inside of the walls and base with clay slurry.
- Use alternate layers about 100mm deep of soft weeds or green waste and dry material. Tread it down lightly.
- Use a layer of bruised and crushed nettles about every 300mm, with a sprinkling of soil.
- Use a 50mm layer of animal manure in the centre.
- Use a light dusting of lime every 300–450mm. Cover it immediately

Biodynamic compost preparations

Preparation	Ingredient	Method	Effect
502	Yarrow blossom (*Achillea millefolium* white form)	Fermented in a male elk or deer bladder for twelve months over winter; it is hung in a tree for six months over summer and autumn (to capture summer influences) before burying for six months over winter (to capture winter influences)	Steiner said that this preparation stimulates plants to use sulphur and potassium more effectively (and this has a flow-on effect to better use of nitrogen)
503	Chamomile flowers (*Matricaria chamomilla*)	Fermented in the small intestines of a cow and buried in humus-rich soil for six months over winter	This preparation is said to 'bring calcium into the right relationship with sulphur' (i.e. helps the plant to use calcium and sulphur more effectively); also said to stabilise nitrogen in manure
504	Stinging nettle (*Urtica dioica*)	Nettle is picked at the flowering stage, placed in a clay pot or pipe and left for twelve months from mid-summer to mid-summer (must go through full solar cycle)	This preparation is said to bring iron into the right relationship with sulphur
505	Oak bark (*Quercus* species). Species with deeply lobed leaves are preferred (e.g. *Q. robur*, English oak)	Made by filling the cranial cavity of a domestic farm animal (cow, pig, sheep, goat or horse) with ground bark and burying in a spot where water trickles through (must be slime and water)	Said to regulate carbon and calcium and to help resist all forms of plant diseases
506	Dandelion flowers (*Taraxacum officinale*)	The flowers are buried inside the mesentery (part of the peritoneum) of a cow over winter in a fertile spot	Said to bring silica into the right relationship with potassium and sulphur
507	Valerian flowers (*Valeriana officinalis*)	Made by squeezing the juice from freshly picked valerian flowers and mixing with lukewarm water and stirring for fifteen minutes*	Said to regulate phosphorus and to assist plants to resist frost damage

**Biodynamic stirring involves alternately stirring in one direction until a vortex is formed, then stirring in the opposite direction so the first vortex collapses and another forms. This process continues for some time, usually 20 minutes.*

with soil or garden waste.
- Finish the heap with a layer of straw.
- Provide shelter from heavy rain.

To encourage rapid composting, use only soft materials such as fresh weeds, kitchen waste of small particle size only, ground nut or flour meals, fruit pomace, fresh autumn leaves, and fresh manure. Keep tougher materials aside for a slower heap or stockpile them until you have enough to hire a shredder.

Ensure the heap starts rapidly by watering it with liquid manure tea (see recipe on pages 74–77) or animal or human urine diluted with 20 times the volume of water, or by using Maye Bruce's herbal preparations. This system can produce useable compost in two months over summer and three months in winter (quicker in tropical regions).

Maye Bruce herbal preparation

Maye Bruce developed the following preparation which bears some similarity to biodynamic preparations but is much easier to make. This version is close to Maye's original instructions, but many local variations exist.

Ingredients

Wild chamomile (*Matricaria chamomilla*)
Common dandelion (*Taraxacum officinale*)
Common valerian (*Valeriana officinalis*)
Yarrow (*Achillea millefolium*)
Stinging nettle (*Urtica dioica*)
Oak bark (*Quercus robur*, English oak)
Pure honey

Method

Gather the flowers and leaves of plants before midday (or earlier in hot weather). For oak bark, use the outer, rougher bark. Keep each herb separate. Dry herbs as soon as possible with slow heat (e.g. hanging the herbs in a room with a combustion heater).

When tinder dry, crush and pass them through a fine wire sieve (a wire kitchen sieve is ideal). Grind or rasp oak bark to powder then pass through the sieve.

Mix 1 teaspoon of honey into half a cup of milk. Make a stock mixture by mixing together equal parts of each ingredient. Mix them thoroughly and store in a covered jar, away from light.

Use

Stir the mixture to an even consistency. Mix 1g (a drop large enough to cover a five cent piece) with 600ml of rainwater. Shake well and let stand for 24 hours.

Once diluted, the mixture will keep for up to three weeks. Shake thoroughly before use.

The short cut

In the above recipe, yarrow and nettle are essential. The other ingredients are claimed to enhance disease prevention and pest control but they can be omitted.

How biodynamic preparations work

Maye Bruce's method and other, similar recipes clearly imitate aspects of the biodynamic method. Some practitioners believe these methods capture vital influences from cosmic inputs. Depending on your belief system, these can be the simple consequence of changing seasonal conditions and nutrients from the soil, or they may be more ethereal.

There are several simple ways these recipes may work, which are quite consistent with a scientific world view. Here are a few:

- The herbs used in these recipes produce root exudates which encourage soil organisms in the root zone. The recipe then contributes these organisms and their food or the compounds that stimulate them. Eventually the soil where BD500 and other preparations are made also becomes a rich breeding ground for soil organisms.

- The recipe imposes a regime on the composter, including use of a variety of construction materials, and rule-of-thumb guidelines that help to achieve a desirable carbon to nitrogen ratio and meet other requirements such as moisture content and aeration.
- The herbs used in these recipes are rich accumulators of nutrients. Many herbs are much richer in trace elements than grasses or clovers. For this reason they are intentionally included in organic pastures. They may also have growth periods that peak at different times, so that at any time of year some of them will be actively growing, and foraging for nutrients.
- The stirring process is a powerful oxygenating method, imitating techniques such as enriched air used to grow cultures in a laboratory. Stirring gives the rich diversity of organisms in the compost a kick-start, causing them to increase in numbers just before the preparation is applied.

Composting in the tropics

Composting in subtropical regions of Australia is similar to temperate regions, except that, if moisture and air are adequate, decomposition happens faster and the process provides finished compost in a shorter time.

Composting in the true tropical zone can be more difficult than in temperate zones. In the wet season, decomposition is very rapid, and high ambient heat helps to drive the process. Large heaps in the tropics can disappear very rapidly into the soil. The benefit is still derived for the soil, but there is less product for other purposes. This is, indeed, the clue to four different approaches to composting in tropical regions:

- deeper mulches and sheet composting
- numerous smaller compost heaps
- covered compost
- compost pits.

Deep mulch and sheet composting

This system acknowledges the rapidity of decomposition in wet and hot conditions and works with nature to deliver humus to the soil surface, where it is needed. Sheet compost is made in layers on the ground, which should be moist before composting begins. The most concentrated products are most appropriately used in the lower levels. Kitchen or fruit waste should be well covered to discourage vermin.

The same rules about C:N ratio apply to sheet composting as to aerobic heaps, so that the composting process occurs *in situ*. Keep building layers, using a variety of available material, and finish with a thick layer of tough or woody material, such as seaweed, straw, tough weed stalks, corn (maize) stalks, or small branches. This process combines the benefits of mulching and composting.

Small compost heaps

Small heaps are made adjacent to where the compost is needed, and the finished product is lightly buried or scratched under the soil surface around crop plants. These small heaps are easy to make from close-to-hand prunings, weeds and leaf litter, pushed up or piled into a heap. They are ready to use in around six or seven weeks.

Covered compost

Covered compost is protected from intense tropical rain and heat. Also, although building compost heaps on concrete is not normally recommended, it can be a useful strategy in the tropics. If made on a concrete slab, the benefits of compost will not be lost to the soil underneath.

If building compost on concrete, you will need to:

- add enough soil or old compost to provide compost micro-organisms
- add earthworms when the thermophilic or hot stage finishes
- monitor other conditions such as moisture and aeration.

Compost pits

This system provides some relief from high temperatures by composting under the ground in a pit. In the pit, temperatures are modified, moisture is conserved and there is high contact with the soil surface on the base and sides of the pit, where the major transition and humification processes are occurring.

Dig a large pit near a tree such as avocado or mango or in the centre of a round vegetable bed and fill with organic matter. The organic matter can simply be left to compost and the heap refilled from time to time. Crop plants send feeding roots into the heap and reap the nutrients directly. Alternatively, the compost may be scraped out of the pit and scattered around or lightly buried under the crop.

Dry tropics

In the dry tropics compost requires monitoring to maintain adequate moisture, which is driven off by intense heat. Thick covers such as carpet squares or underfelt can be used to protect the heap, and shadecloth or metal covers also help. In the dry tropics, large heaps work well as long as moisture is maintained in the heap. Sheet composting and the other techniques mentioned for wet tropics are also appropriate, as is careful attention to mulching to conserve soil moisture.

Compost toilets

Compost toilets recycle nutrients and are waterless. As the toilet is a major contributor to household water use, compost toilets can save a lot of water so they make sense in an arid continent.

Owner-builder designs are readily available, or commercial systems are available from as little as $3,000. Compost toilets are now known and accepted by many local government authorities. National parks in remote and sensitive areas often use compost toilet systems.

Compost toilets need maintenance, however. Some designs require addition of bulking material, such as sawdust, leaves, kitchen waste or shredded paper. Other designs require stirring. Modern commercial compost toilets are more maintenance free than the older designs.

Human waste will have slightly elevated heavy metal levels and may have salt or other residues. After passing through a compost toilet the material should have only very low levels of pathogens, but one mistake could be unfortunate. Faecal wastes potentially carry *Giardia*, hepatitis, bacterial dysentery, amoebic dysentery, cholera and typhoid. Therefore, it is wise to use any compost from the toilet on non-food plants, or at least on tree crops, where soil-applied compost is remote from the harvested land.

8. Composting with worms

'The plough is one of the most ancient and most valuable of man's inventions; but long before he existed the land was in fact regularly ploughed, and still continues to be thus ploughed by earthworms. It may be doubted whether there are many other animals which have played so important a part in the history of the world, as have these lowly organised creatures.'

CHARLES DARWIN, *THE FORMATION OF VEGETABLE MOULD THROUGH THE ACTION OF EARTHWORMS*, 1881

In Charles Darwin's last great biological text he calculated the quantity of soil and organic matter consumed by worms. Darwin wrote: 'Of all animals, few have contributed so much to the development of the world, as we know it, as earthworms.' Aristotle had called them 'the intestines of the earth'. They have also been called 'a mobile humus mill'.

The common garden earthworm is mainly nocturnal, consuming about twice as much during the night as during daytime. Earthworms rarely emerge completely from the ground, unless flushed out during rain, or on rare occasions they may crawl over the soil surface looking for a mate.

Earthworms are omnivores, eating a wide range of food. There are many types of earthworms. Some are suited to gardens, or to composting, and some will only thrive in a natural environment. Some, such as the *Chaetogaster*, are adapted to a specific food, in this case decaying flesh. The largest earthworm is *Megascolecides australis*, or the giant Gippsland earthworm. It can grow to over a metre in length, with 500 segments. Gippsland earthworms make large tunnels with volcano-shaped openings. They can make an odd and very loud sucking sound as they travel through these burrows, pulling their bodies through the airspace and creating a small vacuum behind. Giant earthworm eggs are oval-shaped, measuring about 75 by 20mm.

Earthworms in the garden

The presence of earthworms, measured by the number of individuals, the diversity of species and their activity (or the total amount of material processed), is a good indicator of soil health. To increase the earthworm population in your soil:

- leave raw organic matter, such as straw, seaweed, fresh weeds or autumn leaves, on the soil surface
- avoid overuse of digging
- cover all bare soil with mulch, and
- avoid high nitrogen fertilisers and pesticides.

Earthworms excrete polysaccharides as they tunnel through the soil. Polysaccharides are a form of sugar that glues or sticks soil particles together, preserving earthworm tunnels for many years. The type of earthworms commonly present in Australian gardens mainly move vertically through the soil, dragging bits of organic material underground to feed on. This action helps to mix organic matter into the soil. Any organic material that is eaten by a worm is turned into rich humus, which the worm leaves behind in a 'cast' on the soil surface. Worm casts or castings are also full of micro-organisms that are released into the soil.

Earthworm tunnels aerate the soil and create drainage holes. The earthworm tunnels are lined with the slimy mucus that also covers their bodies. This mucus lubricates their movement, and it also contains polysaccharides and high levels of plant nutrients. Plant roots grow rapidly along these tunnels, utilising the nutrients.

Compost worms

There are about 350 species of earthworms in Australia. Some are found only in undisturbed soil, and some thrive in the garden. Compost worms are quite different from garden worms. Compost worms move quickly over longer distances in search of food, whereas garden worms hardly leave their tunnel, except during the mating season or when they are flushed out by rain, or lack of food.

Three types of compost worm are commonly bred for composting and for fishing. These are tigers, reds and blues. Compost worms require large amounts of organic matter year round, and will not thrive in the garden unless there is deep mulch that is renewed. Composting with earthworms is called vermiculture, from the Latin *vermis* for worm.

Keeping worms

Many different worm-breeding units can be purchased, or a simple system for keeping worms can be easily made from timber or recycled materials. A worm tenement, or multilevel design, is an easy system to manage in a home garden, and can be kept on a balcony. Larger worm pits or heaps can be made from a variety of recycled materials. The worm farm should be located in a shady area, to protect the worms from high temperatures and from drying out.

A typical commercially available plastic worm farm has a collector tray, to catch

Types of earthworms

There are over 3,000 types of earthworms, and at least 350 species live in Australia. Many of these were introduced from overseas. Exotic earthworms do not seem to cause environmental damage, other than some competition with the local species, and indigenous and introduced worms often live happily side by side with no direct conflict.

Native earthworms can be very effective in the garden or in pasture, but introduced compost worms are much faster breeders and rapid processors of concentrated waste. Some common worms include:

Aporrectodea caliginosa A common earthworm in pasture and lightly cultivated soil, in temperate climates. Greyish colour, possibly with a pink head. May also have broad flat areas on the underside.

Lumbricus rubellus Sometimes called a red worm or red crawler. Red in colour, it grows to 100–120mm long. *L. rubellus* is useful in pasture and in compost.

Eisenia fetida Commonly known as the tiger worm. Maximum length is about 100mm. A very useful compost worm, similar in appearance to the red worm, possibly with bands of yellow at the head.

E. andrei Commonly known as the red tiger worm. Very effective compost worm.

It is worth investigating the heap a few days after construction to make sure that it is heating up and moisture is adequate.
(Photo courtesy of Jeff Dale)

Two or three plastic bins can be rotated to give a continual supply of compost. The heap in the foreground has been uncovered to finish maturing.

A well-constructed backyard compost system.

A cut down water tank can be used as a compost bin.

Fungi are an important part of the decomposition cycle. These fruiting bodies are growing out of a straw bale heap.

Plastic conduit with holes drilled into it can be used to aerate large compost heaps.

Hard-to-kill weeds such as those with bulbs or stolons can be pre-rotted in a plastic garbage bin. When the weeds have settled, a solution of weak fish emulsion is added. This brew is added to the compost heap when the problem weeds have anaerobically decomposed.

Straw bales used to retain a compost heap.

This straw bale compost system (or compost 'bin') is covered with plastic during the wetter months to prevent waterlogging. The plastic garbage bin is used to store kitchen waste until a new heap is constructed.

A long-handled fork is an important composting tool.

liquid draining from the upper levels, and several layers of working trays. The first and lowest working tray will need hessian or layers of newspaper spread over the grille, to prevent the worms falling through. Place an upturned ice-cream container or other object in the collector tray, so that any worms falling through can beach, and avoid drowning. Alternatively, use an old rag looped through one of the holes in the grille so that worms can climb back to the working level.

Do not fill the collector tray with compostable material, however. It is only for collecting liquid. The liquid can be drained off through a tap and diluted to make liquid manure suitable for watering pot plants or garden beds.

The first working tray will need suitable worm bedding and worms. Compost worms can be bought from garden centres, fishing outlets and from worm growers, or collected from a friend's compost. They can be purchased as adult worms, or in compost with adult worms, worm eggs and young worms.

To start them off, use old compost, pre-soaked leaf mould or coir (coconut fibre), a few handfuls of soil and well-soaked newspaper. Use at least 8–10cm depth of bedding to start the worms. Add vegetable scraps, manure or weeds a little at a time. Worms need to adjust to a new diet, so do not change their feed rapidly. Introduce new foods a little at a time, and avoid a deep layer of uneaten food, which will putrefy on the surface. The plastic worm farms designed for this purpose and available from garden centres and worm retailers work best with soft organic waste. Feed the worms only organic material that is easily broken down.

When the worms have filled the second level, place the next tray on top, and continue feeding in the third level. The worms will manufacture their own bedding from kitchen waste. The worm farm yields both liquid worm cast and vermicompost.

Occasional additions of lime or wood ashes may be needed to prevent the mix becoming acidic. The best liming materials are eggshells, oyster shells, crushed dolomite and crushed limestone. Do not use garden lime, quicklime, slacked lime, plaster lime or any soda or salt product.

Dry materials may need to be soaked thoroughly before adding. If only

Suitable bedding materials

Cardboard and paper should be shredded and soaked before adding to the farm. Corrugated cardboard can also be used to cover the surface layers of the worm bedding. Don't use heavily waxed cardboard or excessively bleached and coloured paper. Avoid glossy paper.

Leaves make suitable bedding, but use only disease-free leaves. Shredded leaves are preferred — use the lawn mower if you don't have a garden shredder.

Peat moss extraction is usually environmentally destructive, so use other materials in preference. Coir (coconut fibre) or composted sawdust are good alternatives.

Soil is easy to find and cheap but is heavy and dilutes the worm food. It is best mixed with other bedding materials. Professional worm farmers use soil-less bedding. Especially avoid heavy clay soil.

Straw takes a long time to break down but provides a suitable environment. It is best mixed with other material.

Suitable worm food

- Kitchen waste, chopped up to increase surface area
- Tea bags, used tea leaves and coffee grounds
- Bread products and pasta — use only limited quantities of cooked or baked products
- Cracked or ground grain, including wheat, rice and bran, are a preferred food of worms — use these products as a tonic and to promote fast-growing worms
- Pulverised eggshells
- Banana skins and mashed banana
- Weeds and lawn clippings — use only a shallow layer at one time
- Lime (calcium carbonate) — use a thin sprinkling over the top of fresh green waste or kitchen and fruit waste

Unsuitable worm food

- Bones, meat and fish waste
- Dairy products including milk, butter and cheese
- Very oily food
- Large quantities of onion waste added at one time
- Large quantities of very aromatic or strongly scented plants added at one time
- Any organic matter that may have been treated with herbicide
- Quicklime or any strongly reactive alkaline product
- Plastic or other synthetic materials

vegetable scraps are used, the worm farm should not need watering.

Small vinegar flies will sometimes breed in the farm. They are a natural part of the decomposition process. You will encourage houseflies or other pests if you use meat or fish waste in the farm, so dispose of meat by another method.

Some gardeners say that earthworms should not be fed onion waste or citrus skins. These products will be broken down by earthworms but are not their preferred food, so they can be included in small quantities. It is also wise to avoid large quantities of tomato, raw potato and aromatic or strongly smelling plant material such as fennel. The favourite food of earthworms is a high protein diet of cracked and milled grain, and they will grow and multiply rapidly if fed grain and other protein-rich vegetable food. Crack an egg onto the surface of the bedding to witness how attracted worms are to protein. You can use this method to harvest worms from the bedding material, as the egg will encourage them onto the surface. Do not feed them any vegetable waste that may have been sprayed with pesticides.

Earthworms can eat up to their own weight in waste every 24 hours. They have no teeth, but they ingest sand particles which help to grind organic matter in their gizzard. The muscular action of the worm, as it moves through the soil, also helps to grind up its food. Earthworms will have to work less, and therefore will grow and reproduce faster, if their food is easily accessible. Feed them soft food and chop up any large particles. Grind and pre-soak grains.

Earthworms need protection from their natural enemies, which include parasitic flies, birds, small snakes, lizards, frogs, small mammals and marsupials, and the larval and adult stage of some beetles. Worm farms need to be covered with a tight-fitting plastic lid with flyscreens fitted over the air vents. Free heaps can be covered with carpet, underfelt or hessian, and the cover kept moist.

The ideal temperature range for earthworms is 20–25°C. Activity will generally be less at lower or greater temperatures. In warm areas, the worm farm will require shelter from the hot sun. A simple shadecloth roof will suffice. Always leave a suitable depth of organic matter in the farm (at least 8–12cm) so that worms can be buffered against any rapid temperature change, by the insulating value of their bedding. On the other hand, the bedding does not need to be too deep — most compost worms are naturally surface feeders.

Worm farm designs

Many types of containers can be used to contain worms, including old baths, sinks and crates. Inventive worm-growers can use any receptacle that can be adequately drained. The most effective draining mechanism is to insert a small tap, so that the liquid can be drained off. The liquid is a valuable fertiliser and an important product from the worm farm.

Factors to consider in the design of worm farms include:

- controlled temperature range, and avoidance of rapid temperature changes
- adequate moisture — worms require constant moisture to avoid drying out of their 'skin', but are suffocated by over-wet conditions*
- ventilation — worms require oxygen; design airholes in the container and allow air to move freely around the worm farm
- pH — worms require a neutral pH, around pH 7.0. Add lime (calcium

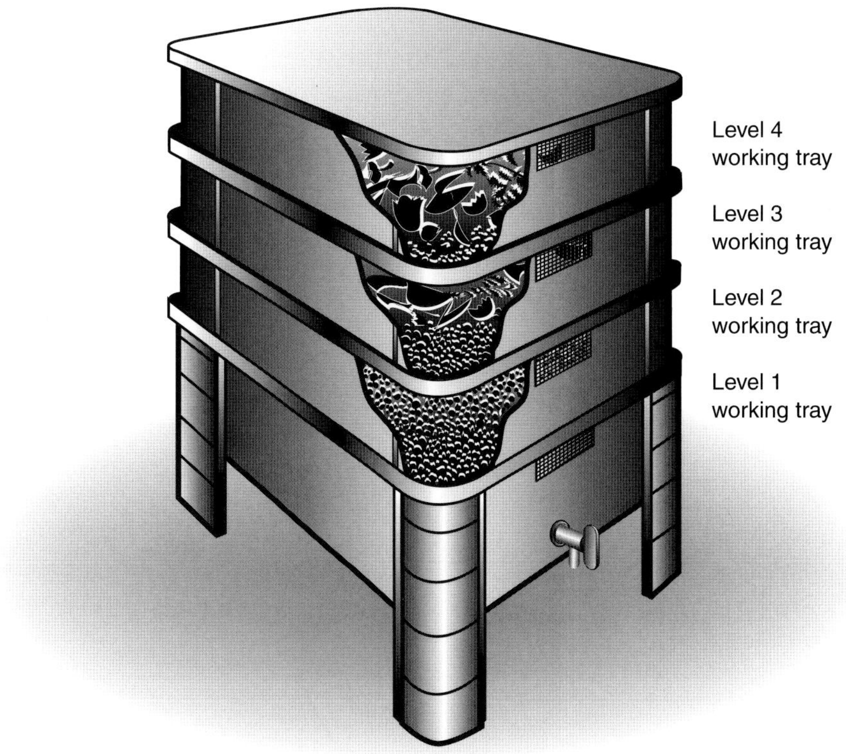

Worm factory

carbonate) or eggshells to balance acidic food waste

- avoid bright light — worms love the dark, and many are mainly nocturnal; use a lid, old blankets or carpet to cover the farm.

* Before using tap water to irrigate worm farms, let it stand for 24 hours (or four hours in bright sun) to allow the chlorine to evaporate.

Polystyrene box

The box needs small holes in the base. Place the worm farm over an empty bucket or other container to capture the valuable liquid. A polystyrene fruit box can hold about 2,000 worms.

Brick enclosure

Build a low brick wall, about 350–500mm high. Layer the worm bedding directly into the enclosure, or use a plastic liner with puncture holes for drainage.

Quentin's vermin-proof waste eliminator

This is a simple and very effective do-it-yourself worm farm designed by Quentin Jones at Nirvana Farm in the Mount Lofty Ranges. The bin is made from a large food-grade plastic barrel, and borrows from the design of compost toilets. A 180 litre pickle barrel or olive barrel is ideal. Quentin has also made wheelie bin versions of the waste eliminator. The advantage of this system is that it is easily and cheaply made at home and is completely enclosed, and therefore vermin proof.

Drill two holes low down on opposite sides of the barrel and fit a piece of 32mm

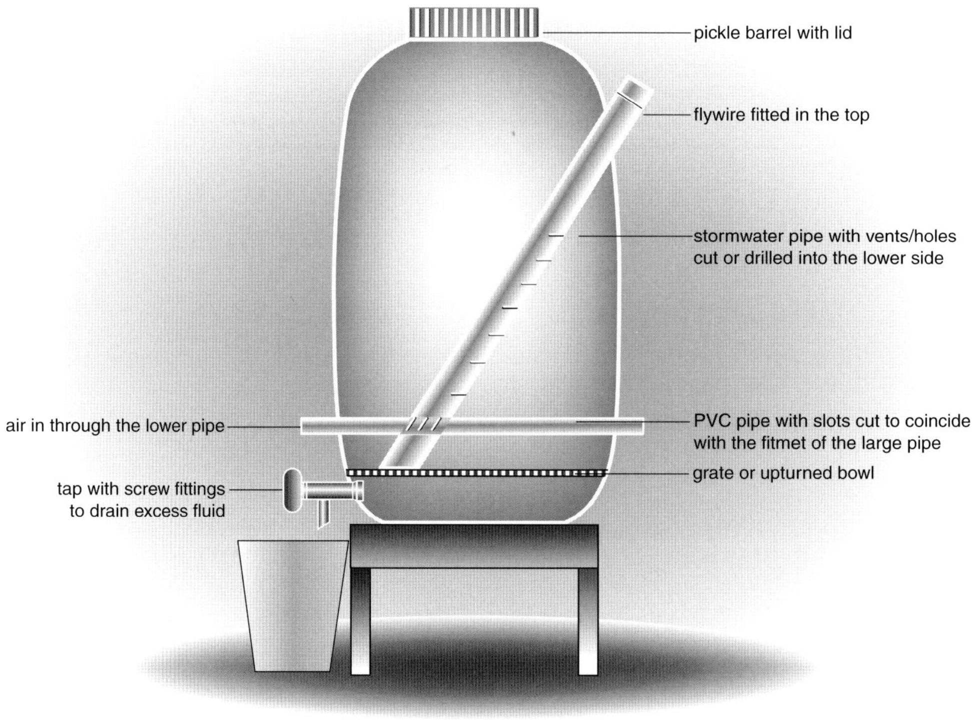

Quentin's vermin-proof waste eliminator

or 40mm PVC conduit through the holes. Cut slots into the conduit to receive the end of a piece of 95/1200mm stormwater pipe, which is passed through a large hole cut near the top of the barrel. The stormwater pipe passes from the top, through the centre of the barrel, finishing at the conduit crosspiece. Cut or drill vents or holes into the stormwater pipe so air can move into the worm bedding, and fit the exposed end of the stormwater pipe with a flyscreen. Drill one more hole close to the bottom of the barrel and fit a poly tap to drain off excess liquid.

Start the system with a grate or upturned bowl placed at the bottom to keep a small well of liquid. Add peat, compost or wet newspaper as bedding, then introduce worms and feed them as required through the tight-fitting lid.

Worm enemies

Worms are preyed on by birds, rodents, small marsupials, reptiles (snakes, lizards and turtles), a variety of insects (mainly ants and beetles), spiders and centipedes, to mention just a few. Centipedes can take a heavy toll on eggs and young hatchlings, as well as adults. Provide basic protection by keeping a lid on the wormery, and by keeping the worms up off the ground.

Using worm castings

Nitrogen (N), phosphorus (P) and potassium (K) are the three nutrients which plants require from the soil in the highest quantity. So-called 'complete' garden fertilisers supply N-P-K, but may not supply a complete range of mineral or trace elements. Earthworm castings usually have a similar or lower N-P-K than compost (about 1-1-1, depending on the source of feed) but they are richer in calcium and trace elements (especially iron, magnesium and sulphur) and bacteria than compost. Use worm castings as you would compost, but remember that any weed seed or plant disease organisms included in the original feed may persist in the vermicompost.

Separating worms from worm bedding

There are many ways of separating worms and bedding material. If you are only using vermicompost in the garden, you may not need to separate the worms — just add them to the garden too. Although compost worms will not thrive in most soil conditions, they will survive under mulch, and even if they do not survive long, they will help to incorporate organic matter added to the soil surface. Eventually their bodies become part of the detritus system.

If you want to separate worms to add back to the next vermicompost, to inoculate the compost heap or for the next fishing trip, try one of the following methods:

Raw egg Crack a raw egg on the surface of the bedding to attract worms that can be scooped up.

Compost piles Remove vermicompost from the worm farm and make piles on a tarpaulin or potting bench. Worms don't like bright light so they will gradually make their way to the bottom of the pile. Scrape off the top layers to harvest compost.

Hand sorting This is a time-consuming but reliable method. Remove one bucket of compost at a time and pick out the worms by hand. Limit the amount of touching because worms are damaged by rough handling and by strong acid on your fingers.

Vermicompost in the home garden

Application	Quantity/frequency	Notes
	Note: These quantities can be used in addition to any normal compost applications	
Lawns	Apply earthworm castings once per year at 20–40kg per 1,000 square metres	Water castings into soil immediately after application
Annual flowers and vegetables	Place a small handful of castings under seeds or around each seedling	Remember that earthworm castings may contain viable weed seed
Perennials	Place a handful of castings into each hole at planting time; apply earthworm castings four times per year at 10–20kg per 1,000 square metres, or once per year at 25–30kg per 1,000 square metres	If possible, cover castings with mulch to prevent them from drying out and to encourage rapid incorporation by soil life
Seed germinating mix	Use earthworm castings up to make up to 25 per cent of the volume of potting soil	25 per cent for gross feeding plants (plants with big feeding requirements)
Potted plants	Mix a handful of earthworm castings into a bucket of potting soil	Remember that castings are more potent than compost, so don't overdo it

Compost sieve Place compost on a layer of mesh and locate a bright light over the top. Provide fresh bedding under the sieve and worms will make their own way down to the new material.

Improving the nutrient analysis of vermicompost

As for any compost, feeding a variety of materials helps to ensure that the finished product will have a reasonable supply of plant nutrients and a full range of trace elements. Grains and other concentrated feeds have a high analysis, but worms fed mainly on a single source of food or nutrient-poor organic matter will produce a much less valuable cast. Horse manure, because it is readily available in outer urban areas, is often used as a source of feed for worm farms, but if it is not mixed with other materials it produces a low-analysis vermicompost. Aged horse manure by itself makes good bedding. However, it is an ideal bedding when mixed with a higher nutrient material.

A valuable way to improve the analysis of vermicompost is to feed finely ground rock flours, hoof and horn manure or bonemeal. Crushed rock flour must be very fine but is a great aid to digestion for the worms, and passing through the worm's gut biologically activates the small rock particles. When they pass out with the cast, they continue working in the soil and provide nutrients to bacteria, fungi and roots. Also see the table on page 56 for a list of source materials for making specific nutritional compost.

Problem solving

Problem	Possible cause/solution
Fruit or vinegar flies	Vinegar flies are not a pest of worms, but may create a minor nuisance by flying around the operator. Avoid flies of all types by burying fresh food under a shallow layer of old bedding. Remove flies from the air with a vacuum cleaner. Make a simple flytrap with beer or other fermenting waste: • Cut the top off a plastic drink bottle and invert the top back into the bottom. • Use tape to connect the two parts of the bottle. • Place bait in the bottom. The flies get trapped inside and drown. • You could also try sticky paper flytraps. Cover worm bedding with old blankets, hessian or carpet. Use flyscreens on plastic farms or keep worms in a screened outbuilding.
Odour	Under ideal conditions the worm farm will not smell and any smelly material added to the farm should cease smelling within 24 hours if lightly buried. For serious odours: • improve ventilation • add calcium carbonate (lime) or crushed eggshells • add zeolite, available from mineral suppliers and garden centres • turn bedding and dry if too wet • reduce depth of bedding (maximum 40–50cm depth) to avoid anaerobic composting.
Grey mould	Mould indicates that too much food has been added at one time. Remove some food (place in compost heap or bin) and add only the amount of food worms can consume in five to seven days.
White thread-like worms	These are enchytraid worms. Not greatly harmful, but they eat worm food. Their presence indicates over-wet or acid conditions.
Worms climbing up the sides and congregating on top of the feed	Ignore if only a few. If many, indicates conditions are not good, generally acid, wet or over-dry conditions, or possibly strong aromatic plants in the bedding.
Worms die off	A variety of factors can cause worms to die: • Temperature. High temperatures (above 32°C) can cause worm death. • Population pressure. Worms will naturally die if they become too crowded. Remove some and start a new wormery, give them to friends, or tuck them under mulch in the garden. • Predators. Nematodes and other predators can invade worm farms. Maintain hygienic conditions, avoid adding soil to bedding, and do not feed more than about five days of feed at one time.

9. Anaerobic composting

Anaerobic composting systems do not require oxygen. A specialised group of organisms are able to survive where there is little free oxygen, and convert organic matter into valuable, nutrient-rich humus or liquid compost.

Anaerobic composting is at work in closed bin systems and composted liquid manures. This type of composting is useful in small gardens with limited room for open heaps but enough space for one or two compost bins tucked into a small corner.

Because anaerobic composts are less efficient at conserving nitrogen than aerobic composts, they can give off bad odours. To avoid these, use a cup full of lime for every 300mm depth of compost. If the smells persist, add zeolite to the compost, which is a natural mined material, available from mineral suppliers and some garden centres.

Plastic compost bins

Plastic compost bins and worm farms are suited to handling a continual supply of kitchen waste which would attract domestic animals and vermin in an open heap. The bins require some management, and there are different schools of thought about how they should be worked. For instance, some people utilise the rodent-proof sides but leave the lid off, and use a slotted pipe down the centre to get the compost working aerobically. Others use the bins as they were intended, to produce anaerobic compost.

To use this method, press the bin into the soil. Start the bin off with some 'biscuits' broken off a bale of hay — lucerne hay is ideal. The hay will absorb liquid coming off moist kitchen waste. Add a handful of soil and a sprinkling of lime or fine dolomite to each bucket of kitchen waste.

Keen composters usually need two or three bins, one to fill with current compost and another maturing. While the bin is maturing you cannot really add new material to it, otherwise when you lift the bin, partly decomposed waste is exposed to rodents, flies and dogs. Leave the compost to mature when the bins are full. New material should go into a fresh bin, with more soil, lime or dolomite and thin layers of lawn clippings. Take care to thinly sprinkle lawn clippings to avoid matted, slimy and smelly layers.

When the load has stopped shrinking, the bin can be removed and the heap, moulded to the shape of the bin, but now reduced to about one-third of the height, is left to mature further before being used on garden beds. This system is pretty much what the manufacturer intended, and is ideal for small, space-conscious gardens.

Ivor Patch, an 85-year-old gardener from Melbourne, has developed a system for managing with only one plastic bin. Ivor is space conscious, and is also keen on economy. He has a productive and attractive garden which benefits from ample compost. Ivor digs the bin deeply into the soil, a good idea for rodent control because they will tunnel under the bin if it is buried too shallow. When the bin is full, he removes it from the heap, burying it again close by. The top of the old heap goes into the bottom of the new bin, and the rest of the old heap is left to mature. All this happens in the same location, next to a separate aerobic compost and leaf mould, so the soil is easy to dig and is continuously benefiting from the new organic matter.

Plastic compost bins can also be used as worm farms, with the lid off and covered with hessian. Ivor Patch's system may also enhance worm involvement. They can come up into the bin from underneath and the hessian cover allows a good oxygen supply.

Plastic bins can also be used to store kitchen scraps until a large aerobic heap is built.

Plastic garbage bags

Some people use plastic garbage bags as a simple way to make compost. The bags are filled with organic matter and lime, together with blood and bone or a 'complete' organic fertiliser, at the ratio of one handful of blood and bone, two cups of lime and several litres of water per large garbage bag. Because oxygen is limited the composting process is slow, and the contents may smell if the bag is disturbed before composting has finished.

Plastic bags are also suitable for holding vegetable scraps until enough material is accumulated to make a compost heap. If they are to be kept for longer than three weeks, treat them as described above.

Liquid manures

Organic growers sometimes use liquid manure preparations. They are useful if correctly made and applied, but may contravene organic principles and organic certification rules if misused or not prepared correctly.

Liquid manures from animal by-products could be made from material which has first been aerobically composted. Composting 'brought in' organic matter before use is recommended to assist with garden hygiene and to remove biological contaminants and pathogens.

Anaerobic composting in a drum is another suitable system for preparing liquid manure. There are numerous different recipes, and many keen gardeners have their favourite brew. Here is a simple recipe:

- Place manure or fish waste in a plastic or metal drum to one-third full.
- Fill the container with water and stir.
- Cover the drum with a lid to prevent excessive loss of ammonium and to keep out flies and other pests.
- Stir the mixture in the container once every three days and preferably at least

Hints for use of plastic compost bins

- Always use the bins directly on the soil.
- Use a cup of lime or dolomite and several cups of soil on top of each 10–15cm layer of vegetable waste.
- Use green matter such as fresh lawn clippings, but use them sparingly. Distribute only a thin layer of clippings so they do not form a matted barrier.
- When the bin is full, allow the material to finish composting for at least three weeks before removing the bin, and then several weeks to cure after that.
- Use the compost anywhere it is needed. You do not have to dig it in, just place it on the soil surface and allow the worms to do the digging for you.

once per week. An exception to this may be to stir daily for the first three days and then leave for weekly intervals.

- When the smell has gone the manure is ready for use. The mixture will smell when first made and the container should be located where it is least likely to cause offence. A strong but less offensive smell may be evident directly over the barrel but the penetrating ammonium smell that develops shortly after the liquid manure is mixed should no longer be present. Maturation usually takes four to five weeks, depending on weather conditions and the ingredients.
- Apply the liquid manure in a diluted form in watering cans or through drippers via a venturi watering valve.

The rate and frequency of use are highly dependent on individual circumstances, including whether the crop is a heavy feeder, the soil nutrition and the application method. Generally, however, a very dilute mixture can be applied once per week or a less dilute application every two or three weeks.

Overusing liquid manure can add high levels of nitrogen not in keeping with good organic nutrition or soil development. Careful use is required.

Method for making liquid manure

Liquid manure from plants

A safer system that avoids the potential overuse of nitrogen from using liquid manure from animals is to make the liquid from green plants. The result is still called liquid manure and is made the same way, except that the drum is loosely filled right to the top with plants, and then water is added to cover them.

Nettles and comfrey make excellent liquid manures but any actively growing green herbaceous plant can be used, including freshly cut weeds. If you are lucky enough to live near a beach, washed up kelp is well worth collecting for this purpose, or for the compost heap. Other

Liquid fertiliser from weeds and seaweed

- Loosely fill a large plastic drum or metal drum with weeds, fill with water and cover.
- Stir every two to four days.
- Leave to mature for at least two or three weeks, or until any pungent ammonium smells have disappeared.
- Filter the liquid and dilute with water at least three to one.
- Apply to plants or soil.
- The mixture can be reused by simply leaving the solids in the drum and topping up with water. After the second time, toss the old weeds into the compost. See also compost tea on page 85.

seaweeds are also useful, but kelp is best. You may need a permit to collect from your local council. Some organic and biodynamic gardeners grow herbs such as stinging nettles, comfrey, yarrow, chamomile and valerian specifically for making liquid fertiliser or adding to the compost.

Using liquid fertilisers

Foliar fertilisers, such as liquid seaweed and manure, are absorbed through plant leaves. They may also be applied to soil, but are most often applied directly to foliage. When used every two to four weeks during the main growth period, they are a good way to provide an extra boost of nutrients and growth hormones, just when the plants need them. Foliar fertilisers can supply nutrients when they are missing from the soil, or unavailable because of chemical 'tie-up' in the soil, or when roots can't take them up due to cold soil temperatures or stress.

Some foliar fertilisers are an excellent source of micro-nutrients, especially the products that are made from kelp. The fish emulsion products are also a good source of micro-nutrients. These days there are many high-tech liquid fertilisers that can deliver a precise amount of nutrients in different mixtures. Although these are very good for correcting production problems, the simple, old-style seaweed fertilisers still have a role to play as general tonic and trace element snacks for the plant.

If you want to remain totally organic, observe the label on purchased products closely and avoid the products that have very high nitrogen levels.

Critical times for the use of foliar fertilisers are:

- on very young plants, when the plant hormones greatly assist root development
- unseasonal cold spells early in the growing season, when soil temperatures are too low for roots to work effectively
- peak growth or stress periods, such as the lead-up to flowering and fruit set.

Leaf crops can tolerate dilute applications every two weeks. Take care not to use a sprayer that has previously been used for herbicides. Set the nozzle to a fine spray.

The best time to spray is early morning, otherwise spray in the late afternoon. An overcast day is fine, but not if rain is expected. Avoid applying foliar fertilisers in very cold or very hot weather, as leaves 'close down' during extreme temperature conditions and won't make use of the beneficial nutrients you are applying. Apply the fertiliser until the leaves are dripping, and remember there will be more open pores on the underside than on top, so spray the underside as well.

Foliar fertilisers can be used to drench the roots of plants that are stressed by weather or disease, or when they are recovering from transplanting. They can also be used through irrigation drippers, although some fish emulsion products have too many solids to work well in this way.

Good kelp-based seaweed fertiliser supplies about 60 nutrients that plants need. It also contains plant hormones, vitamins and enzymes, which play a role in regulating functions such as flowering, root extension and branching. They are quite safe in the recommended dose.

You can also purchase powdered kelp, which is a great slow-release, leach-resistant fertiliser. The powder can be added directly to the soil or to compost, or sprinkled on worm farms to improve the nutrient analysis of the vermicompost.

10. Solving compost problems

Basic compost is simple to make. As your experience grows, you will be able to handle more difficult materials. Many common compost problems are easily solved. This chapter offers suggestions on how to recognise and remedy compost problems.

Some easy solutions

The smell of ammonia could mean too much nitrogen, a pH level that is too high, a saturated or too tightly packed heap. Overcome this problem by opening and rebuilding the heap or mixing in extra carbon-containing material.

Too much moisture will lead to pools of water around the heap, soggy compost or putrid smells. Turn the heap slowly over for a few hours on a warm day to dry it out. Then cover the heap with a tarpaulin, corrugated iron or biscuits of hay to prevent further over-wetting from rain.

In heaps with very smelly ingredients, such as fish waste, natural zeolite can be added to the heap to control odour. Add the equivalent of 2–4 per cent of the volume of the heap. Zeolite is available from garden centres or mineral suppliers.

If the pile does not decompose it may be suffering from excessive dryness, poor aeration, lack of nitrogen or because of special characteristics of the site. Heaps built under coniferous trees often compost very poorly, because the resins that drip off the needles inhibit the growth of composting organisms. A small quantity of needles in the heap will still compost, after some time, but the constant input of new turpines and phenols from the dripline will severely affect the composting process.

An extra word on rats and mice

If rats invade the compost, you may need to review the inclusion of vegetable wastes, or the design of the heap. In a well-made compost heap, the edible vegetable wastes should be converted to an unattractive form within 24 to 48 hours. If this is not happening, it could be a result of:

- inadequate nitrogen
- inadequate bulk, which means the heap is not heating
- using too-large vegetable particles
- inadequate moisture.

To solve these problems turn and repack the heap to ensure food wastes are buried deeply, and do not add meat or fish waste. If rats are persistent, cease adding vegetable scraps to the heap. Instead, use a sealed worm farm or bin for meat and fish wastes.

Quick guide to problem-solving

Problem	Cause	Solution
Ants	Heap is too dry	Ants will reform and remix the heap. They do not damage the compost. Wet the compost and the ants will move out.
Anaerobic odour	Excess moisture	Turn the heap to improve drainage and add dry leaves.
	Heap too large	Rebuild heap to smaller dimension.
	Temperature greater than 55°C	Open heap out and mix in carbon materials.
	Compaction	Turn the heap.
Ammonia odour	Too much nitrogen	Add carbon-containing material (e.g. dry leaves, shredded paper, wood shavings, straw).
Flies	Small vinegar flies are a natural part of the compost process and cause no real harm.	Tolerate vinegar flies if possible as they contribute to the compost process.
	House flies are also a natural part of the decomposition process, but they cause more nuisance and may transmit disease.	Cover organic wastes with a thin layer of soil or mature compost. Avoid adding meat, fish, dairy food or manure wastes.
High temperature	Heap too large	Reduce windrow size.
Low temperature	Heap too small	Combine heaps to make larger.
	Insufficient moisture	Water the heap.
	Poor aeration	Turn the heap to incorporate air.
Maggots	Meat, fat, fish waste or faeces	Remove the cause, cover maggots with lime and cover the heap with a layer of soil. Turn the heap, and make it larger and hotter.
Rodents	Using meat and vegetable scraps without sufficient burying	If rats invade compost, turn and repack the heap. Ensure food wastes are buried deeply. Do not add meat waste. If rats are persistent, cease adding vegetable scraps.
	Rats may also build homes in a warm winter heap	Use traps or baits, or encourage cats or dogs to hunt.
	Rats in plastic compost bins	Bury the bin 150–200mm into the soil. Line the base with aviary wire.

A straw mulch protects the shallow root systems of lettuces from harsh climatic extremes.

Mulch is an important part of soil management in the vegetable garden.

Comfrey produces large amounts of organic matter that can be harvested for compost, mulch or liquid manure. Here, comfrey is growing in a potato patch, where it provides a continuous supply of on-site mulch.

Mulch gardens are an excellent way of building healthy soil. Here, gypsum, lime and blood and bone have been spread on the soil before laying out a thick newspaper mulch. This will be covered with compost and straw.

Plastic mulch is used to suppress weeds and prevent drying out on these high planting mounds.

Dolichos (*Dipogon lignosus*) is a useful green manure legume for the tropics. (Photo courtesy of Allen Gilbert)

Soya beans are grown for their high-protein beans, and their value as a green manure for the soil. (Photo courtesy of Allen Gilbert)

Legumes such as strawberry clover are used as green manure crops to enrich the soil. (Photo courtesy of Allen Gilbert)

White clover is a common legume that has naturalised in many lawns and gardens. Its nitrogen-fixing root nodules add nutrients to the soil. (Photo courtesy of Allen Gilbert)

Broad beans, usually grown as a winter bean crop, make excellent green manure as the plants are both bulky and good nitrogen fixers. The flowers are also attractive and loved by bees. (Photo courtesy of Allen Gilbert)

This field of lupins is ready to be ploughed back into the soil where it will decompose, adding valuable organic matter and nitrogen. (Photo courtesy of Allen Gilbert)

Lupins and marigold growing side by side in the home vegetable plot. (Photo courtesy of Allen Gilbert)

Quick guide to problem-solving (cont.)

Problem	Cause	Solution
Slow decay	C:N balance incorrect	Add more nitrogen (e.g. blood and bone).
	Pile too small	Increase size of heap by adding more material.
	Lack of oxygen	Turn heap to incorporate air, use slotted conduit or other methods to get air in.
	Not enough water	The heap should be moist but not sodden — water the heap with a gentle spray.
	Too much water	Turn the heap to improve drainage, add dry leaves.
	Too cold in winter	Cover the heap with carpet or hessian or make the heap larger. Use hot manures such as pigeon or poultry. These are high in nitrogen and sugars. Insulate the heap with thick biscuits of straw.
Spiders	Natural part of compost process	Wolf spiders and other ground-dwelling hunting spiders often live in compost, so tolerate them as much as possible. Web-making spiders, including red-backs, may nest under the lid of plastic compost bins or on worm farms. Use a handle on the lid, wear gloves and check under the lid before handling. Brush webs and spiders away. Remember that spiders are part of the natural biodiversity of your garden, and kill many plant pests.
Soggy, wet compost	Too much rain	Cover the heap with tarpaulins or plastic sheets.
	Too much irrigation	Turn the heap to improve drainage and add dry leaves. Leave the heap open during the day to increase drying and turn the heap over slowly for several hours.

11. Using compost

'Lay on more compost, and fallow again.'
Thomas Tusser, 1557

Compost is a valuable additive for building soil productivity and health. It also requires time and energy to make, so it should be used carefully to ensure that the maximum value is obtained. Compost may be:

- dug into the soil
- used as surface mulch
- made into a liquid preparation, or
- used in potting soil.

Matured compost

If possible, only use compost that is fully matured. Sometimes compost is required as mulch before it is completely finished. Do not bury immature compost into the root zone of plants, especially young seedlings. During the decomposition process, the powerful organic acids and other chemicals released can prevent germination of seeds and hinder plant growth.

Mature compost is dark in colour, crumbly and completely homogenised, with the sweet smell of good earth. By homogenised we mean that all the material looks similar, and almost all of the original ingredients can no longer be recognised. Sometimes an acorn, a leaf or other organic matter will survive as a recognisable entity through a 'hot' compost pile. When rubbed in the fingers, however, it will generally disappear to homogenous black smudgy particles.

Applying compost

Compost is used at or near the surface of the soil. Very rarely is it necessary to dig it in to a depth greater than a few centimetres. Incorporating compost into soil is best done by lightly tickling it into the surface with a rake, hoe or weeding fork. Compost placed on or near the surface will be gradually buried by worms and other soil animals.

If unfinished compost or raw organic matter is used only at the surface, any plant-inhibiting chemicals released during the early stages of decay will be diluted by the volume of soil underneath. Many books recommend never using partly finished compost, because it ties up nitrogen reserves in the soil. This is only true if the compost is fully incorporated into the soil. Compost only needs to be dug in deeply to quickly develop or renovate a garden bed for perennials or deep-rooted annual vegetables, and in certain specialist uses, such as establishing a permanent asparagus bed or when planting a tree.

Spreading the compost as mulch is quite adequate. The compost will slowly work its way into the soil, by rolling into the spaces, or earthworms and other soil creatures may pull it down. This is the natural way that most organic matter enters soil, except for roots, which die and rot *in situ*. Under the compost mulch, immediately at the soil surface, a layer of soil organisms will thrive. They will integrate the goodness of the compost into the soil over the season, without the need to disturb roots or labour over cultivation.

Just beneath the soil surface is the zone of maximum decomposition. This is known as the rotting fence principle: kick an old fence post and it will break not at the soil surface, but just below, at the zone where soil organisms have uninhibited access to oxygen, and enough shelter from sun and the effects of temperature.

If soil is exposed to sun or wind, cover the compost layer with less valuable mulch to protect the compost from drying out. Because compost is a valuable product, it is worth protecting the compost with another layer of mulch as a normal practice. This extra layer may not be necessary under trees, where the compost is shaded from bright sunlight and protected from washing away by strong rain. In other locations, the dark colour of compost may contribute to the aesthetic appeal of the garden. Where the applied compost is exposed to the elements, a thin covering of straw or other mulch will help to protect and keep soil organisms active at the soil surface.

Quantity of compost

Few of us are able to produce all the compost we would like. Adding about 20–40mm of compost each year in one or two applications would be ideal for most vegetable gardens. Compost may be spread thinly, and still benefit the soil, but larger quantities are of even greater benefit. Best practice would be to spread 20mm of compost onto vegetables, flowers or other crops once or twice per year, but few of us have access to this quantity of product for the whole garden. If you have much less and want to spread it evenly around the garden, make a mixture in the watering can and water it onto the soil (not the plants). This will improve the effectiveness of a small amount and is better than dry broadcasting a thin layer. Remember to remove the rose from the spout of the watering can.

Avoid putting so much compost on one spot that it smothers existing roots. Smothering depth will vary with plant species, soil type and climate, but generally 20–40mm of compost applied at one time is enough. More than twice that amount could well limit oxygen movement into the soil. Better to make the upper layers of mulch from material that packs loosely and allows air to pass through, such as straw, hay, seaweed, wood shavings or bark chips.

Compost in potting soil

Do not use pure compost for potted plants. However, compost or leaf mould does make an excellent ingredient or component of potting mix. From 25–33 per cent of a potting soil can be compost. The remainder can be other good potting soil ingredients, such as bark and sharp sand.

Lawns

To prepare the bed for sowing a new lawn, mix a thick layer of compost into the top 15cm of soil. On established lawns, apply compost twice per year in a layer no thicker than 10mm, and water it in well.

Compost should always be added to new soil brought in to create a lawn. Brought-in soil has probably come from a quarry or pit, and not from the soil surface layer. It may have plant nutrients but probably does not contain soil organisms and their by-products, which stimulate and support healthy plant growth.

While lawn clippings make an excellent compost ingredient, it is also worth considering leaving some clippings on the lawn to rot. This is easy if you purchase a mulching mower, which chops the clippings up into small pieces, or if you pass over the lawn several times with a mower, to re-chop loose clippings.

Trees and shrubs

Place a layer of compost up to 25mm deep around the base of trees and shrubs extending out to the drip line. Push the compost away from the trunk or stem to avoid encouraging stem rot.

For better weed control, place a continuous, overlapping layer of cardboard or newspaper on the soil first. To protect the compost, you may wish to cover with mulch that is in a more raw state, such as straw. Compost can safely be applied to most trees and shrubs once or twice per year.

To prepare soil for new plantings of trees and shrubs, dig to a depth of 250mm, or at least twice the width of the root ball. Apply compost to the bottom of the hole and mix more compost thoroughly into the soil as the hole is refilled around the roots of the new plant.

Sieving compost

Good-quality finished compost may not need screening but in some situations it is useful to screen compost, especially when:

- the dog buries bones in the heap
- lots of rough woody material was used in the heap, and some remains uncomposted
- other difficult materials remain undecomposed in the heap.

An excellent system is to set up a sieve that fits over the garden barrow, an easy task for the home handy person. The best designs have handles on each end so two people can hold and shake the sieve to encourage material through. A single-person operation can be improved by having the sieve slope down towards you. After throwing the compost against the mesh, gravity moves it down and through the sieve. Large objects slide off the end. Gentle agitation with a compost fork or shovel can help material work down through the mesh.

An old mesh-based bed frame also makes a reasonable sieve. They can be purchased cheaply from recycling centres. Smaller hand-held garden sieves are fine for small volumes.

Compost tea

See Chapter 9 for a description on how to make liquid manure. Compost tea is a similar product, made from finished compost. It is a useful soil tonic and an excellent way to spread the benefit from a small amount of compost over the whole garden.

Simply place compost in a bucket or drum until about one-half to two-thirds full, fill with water, and allow to soak for eight hours, if agitated occasionally, or 24 hours if agitated only a few times.

Alternatively, place compost in a hessian sack and suspend the bag in a drum of water. Agitate the liquid two or three times on the first day and every day or two for a week. The compost will be ready to use after a week of soaking, or a few days if agitated more often. Some gardeners advocate more rapid stirring of the brew immediately prior to using, to get a suspension of nutrients and organisms. Do not leave the tea brewing for longer than one month.

Decant the mixture to a watering can or spray unit and dilute with four times its volume of water. The finished compost tea should be a light amber colour, similar to the colour of weak tea. If it is a much darker colour, dilute it with more water.

You can use compost tea safely anywhere in the garden. It is particularly useful for:

- newly planted seedlings or transplants
- sick or unthrifty plants in need of a tonic
- any potted plants — use at least three or four times per year, not more often than once every three weeks, during the main season of growth
- lawns — apply three or four times per year during the growing season
- the vegetable patch — apply once every three or four weeks during the growing period.

The used compost can be resoaked several times if you add a little fresh compost each time. The compost residue is still potent as a soil additive. Use it as mulch or place it around the roots of young seedlings, as you would fresh compost.

Compost tea should be used when growing conditions are good, but do not use in very cold or hot weather. In summer, apply in early morning or late afternoon, when plant stomates — the openings in the leaf surface — are open. Broadleaf and tree crops have stomata on the underside, so the underside will need to be thoroughly covered for foliar applications to be effective. Use a little liquid seaweed fertiliser to make the compost tea adhere to leaves better.

Compost spray

Some compost has been found to be very useful for disease control when sprayed onto susceptible plants. Because compost contains a wide range of living micro-organisms, some are competitive with or antagonistic to disease organisms. In Europe, research has concentrated on the use of tree-bark compost for preventing fungal diseases.

For decades, organic gardeners have used simple compost sprays to help control black spot and other diseases. Although there is little experimental research into this technique to back up anecdotal success, if common sense is used then there is little opportunity for harm when spraying.

To make a compost spray for disease control, agitate a 1kg ice-cream container of compost in a bucket of water for fifteen minutes, then spray directly onto diseased plants, or use as a disease preventative for damping off and other fungal diseases of seedlings.

Storing compost

Compost is best used when mature, and can be kept for several years under ideal conditions. The heap will continue to shrink in volume, and will leach nutrients if too wet. Place the heap away from invasive tree roots on a thick layer of cardboard or on a weed mat or shadecloth placed on the soil. Cover the heap with a layer of straw or weeds to encourage some reworking of the heap by earthworms. The final step is to cover the heap with a water-shedding layer. This could be a tarpaulin, black plastic, or straw biscuits laid very thickly. If using an oxygen-inhibiting layer, like plastic, place timbers or spacers under the sheet to lift it slightly above the heap and allow some air in. Every few months check the heap for moisture.

There is always an exception

Adam Voysey, a compost gardener from Mylor in South Australia, grows in a 100 per cent mature compost. Conventional wisdom says that after 30 per cent compost inclusion in potting soils, or in the top 15cm of soil, the main plant feeding zone, there is little additional benefit from more compost. It is important to stress that Adam grows in completely matured compost, which has finished working and aged for three months. To use younger or less mature compost as the only growing medium could be unhealthy.

Adam began his experiments by ordering a large load of certified organic compost. He prepared his garden in raised beds 400mm high.

When the organic compost is delivered, Adam gives it a light sprinkle with water and lets it sit in the same pile for one month to complete its composting process. Then he shovels the compost directly into the raised beds, to an average depth of around 350mm, and allows it to settle for a day. Once the compost has settled, Adam sprays the beds with a hose and ensures that they stay nicely moist for a period of around three weeks in summer and six to eight weeks in winter. After this time the compost will 'wet nicely' and should be evenly damp throughout with a 'nice earthy smell'.

Following the final heavy watering, the bed is left to sit unturned for a fortnight, after which time it is ideal for the first crop. Only the top 5cm of the bed are raked over prior to the first planting.

Adam says the first crop can be sown as seed, but the germination will be down on expected levels because of the richness of the compost 'soil'. In light of this it is probably better to use seedlings rather than seed at this early stage. Adam also suggests that the first crops should be gross feeders, such as cabbage or sweet corn, to take the edge off the richness for the subsequent second crop.

During the time the first crop is growing there is some 'shrink back' from the sides of the beds, which perhaps indicates that the compost is still finishing its breakdown process. Adam suggests it is necessary to work the soil for the next crop, at which time the excellent evolving soil structure is evident. Following the first crop the shrinkage factor is virtually over, and the soil is ideal for direct sowing seed for any crop.

Compost can also be kept in plastic rubbish bins, which are useful for storage in the potting shed. Add water or dilute seaweed fertiliser if the material dries out.

Compost cautions

Do not store compost when it is too wet. Always wear a facemask and ensure adequate ventilation if moving wet compost. *Legionella* and other undesirable organisms will not thrive in well-cared-for compost, but may be a problem in wet, musty conditions. People who are already ill, with a low immune response or respiratory infection should take extra precautions when handling compost, especially dry compost that can create a dust or aerosol (air suspension).

Do not store compost on a creek bank, or in locations where accidents, stock or weather can move it into streams. Use care when applying compost to sloping surfaces, during the wet season or with spray or flood irrigation. Large amounts of organic matter at one time are not good for waterway ecology. Unfinished compost may contain toxic water-soluble organic chemicals.

12. Green manure

The term 'green manure' refers to a crop grown specifically for ploughing or turning back into the soil. When green manures are mainly used for the purpose of soil protection, they may also be called 'cover crops' or 'ley' crops. Green manures are usually turned in when still green and fresh, or while they are still actively growing. They may also be slashed or mulched and left on the soil surface, rather than incorporated. Organic best practice also recommends their use between productive crops, for a period of between two and six months every year.

Green manures are useful for many reasons. They:

- provide organic matter and humus to the soil
- prevent excess nitrates leaching from the soil
- maintain soil cover as an alternative to fallowing and to prevent erosion
- improve the physical condition of the soil
- assist in the control of weeds and as an extra rotation for the control of plant diseases.

When to use green manure

Green manure is a very economical source of organic matter. It can be produced on site, at almost no cost. Other manures must be purchased or collected, and hauled to the garden. Lush green manure also looks better than bare soil or invasive weeds.

- Use green manure when developing a new garden to prepare the soil for the flower and vegetable crops to follow.
- Green manure is particularly useful for developing new gardens in heavy clay or very sandy soils.
- Use green manure if you are applying raw, uncomposted animal manures, or heavy applications of mineral fertilisers, to encourage these inputs to become thoroughly integrated into the soil, before planting a food crop.
- Use fast-growing, competitive green manure crops to smother bothersome weeds.
- Use green manure as an integral part of a fertility building program for poor soil.
- Use green manure or cover crops as a form of soil cover any time that annual garden beds are not being used for main crops, for a period of six weeks or more, including over the winter months.
- Use green manure occasionally to rest intensively cropped land, for a period of at least two to six months.
- Green manures can help dry boggy soil, especially in warm and humid climates.

Choice of species

Many species are suitable for use as a green manure. The right crop for each situation will depend on environmental conditions, including soil moisture and temperature, and the particular reason for using a green manure crop.

A green manure crop must:

- suit local soils and climate
- provide a large quantity of humus-forming material in the cropping time available
- be able to compete with weeds.

Remember that a large root system is as important and useful as a mass of above-ground growth. Many commonly recommended green manures have vigorous root systems, which can:

- exploit a large area of soil for nutrients (to be recycled to the following crop in a plant-available form)
- open up or loosen the soil
- encourage microbial life in the soil (to maintain the soil ecosystem)
- contribute large quantities of organic matter to the soil when they die.

Legumes (nitrogen-fixing plants) and non-legumes are suitable for use as a green manure. A mixture of different species, including legumes and non-legumes, is also suitable and may return a better mix of nutrients to the soil.

If practicable, it is a good idea to correct any known nutrient deficiencies before planting a green manure crop. Good fertility at the start will be rewarded with increased growth, and nutrients will be conserved and recycled.

Green manure crops will also interact with other crops in the rotation program. For instance, they can provide a disease break, or alternatively, a disease carry-over. Choice of green manure may vary depending on the nutritional demand of preceding and following crops. For example, all legumes are in the same family as peas and beans. They are better suited to preceding a cabbage crop than a crop of peas or beans. Mustard and canola are members of the cabbage family, so they should not be used immediately prior to a brassica crop.

Getting it right

Here are a few questions to ask when planting a green manure.

- How long will the ground be available?
- What are the green manure crop choices for this season (refer to table on pages 93–96)?
- What does the crop need to cope with (for example, frost, drought, etc.)
- Which of the benefits of green manure are most needed for the soil type and condition?
- How will the green manure choice relate to other aspects of crop rotation (for example, disease carry-over or nutrient demand)?
- What will the next crop be?

Planting green manure

Planting a green manure is easy. Pull or chip weeds, rake the ground so it is level, and sow the seed as broadcast or in drill holes. It is not necessary to fertilise most green manure crops or add compost, although you could choose to do this on poor ground.

Turning in

Green manures should generally be turned in while still green and actively growing, or before the crop reaches maturity and produces seed (see exceptions listed on page 92). If non-legumes are used it may be necessary to supply a little additional nitrogen to speed decomposition, by the use of composted manure or liquid compost at the time of ploughing in. Avoid overcultivating when turning manure crops in.

If the temperature is warm enough, the moisture supply is adequate and the green manure crop is still succulent, succeeding vegetable crops may be planted about three to six weeks later. If any of these conditions are lacking, the manure crop may take longer to thoroughly break down. Planting too early carries the risk that by-products of the decay process will damage tender young seedlings or transplants.

Chopping the green manure before incorporating into the soil will speed the time required for decomposition. Crops over 16cm tall can be slashed first to make turning in easier.

Do not turn green manures in too deeply. They should decompose rapidly in the presence of air. Anaerobic decomposition may occur if the trash is buried too deep. The resulting decomposition will be slower, conserve less nitrogen and the humus manufactured may not last as long in the soil.

If you select green manure species that do not regrow from the roots, they do not have to be turned in to the soil. Just cut them to the soil surface and let them decompose there. Any standing crop, including weeds, can be used in this way to provide the benefits of green manure. This method will work even underneath trees, shrubs or vines. Some green manures, such as sorghum, Japanese millet and clover, can be cut several times during their vegetative growth phase to increase production of organic matter. Mowing later in the growth cycle kills Japanese millet and sorghum, but clovers may need to be lightly tilled in.

Sometimes crops with a defined seasonal growth pattern are selected as cover crops. They are then allowed to be killed by cold, or to finish their growth period and naturally die on site, and effectively become mulch. Some winter-growing grasses and clovers are reliably killed by the high temperatures reached in late spring or early summer. If winter growth was vigorous, a good bulk of plant mass will dry off and become summer mulch.

If properly managed, green manure provides excellent soil-improvement benefits for subsequent crops.

Green manure crops:

- keep the ground covered and so prevent erosion
- keep biological activity going by protecting soil life from extremes of weather
- capture and retain nutrients by preventing run-off and leaching loss, especially of nitrogen
- increase water infiltration and reduce surface ponding
- make nutrients available to subsequent crops as they decompose
- loosen and aerate the soil, especially the deep-rooting species
- make clay soils more friable
- improve drainage and infiltration
- improve water holding in sandy soils and so reduce irrigation and lengthen the growing season
- smother weeds, especially the fast-growing, competitive species
- add attractiveness to land that would otherwise be bare
- add useful organic matter that will eventually produce humus in the soil
- build healthy soil structure.

Green manure in small gardens

Green manure crops take up space, but the benefits of green manure can still be obtained by more intimately integrating them into the garden. Selectively hand-pull weeds to allow self-germinating clovers to grow between larger plants such as corn, and longer-growing plants such as old varieties of brassica. Taller-growing plants can also be used, if cut regularly and used to mulch the main crop.

Spot planting

Try planting green manure in those bare spots in the garden. Use peas, beans, clovers, rye-grass or any other fast-growing plants to fill vacant patches before the weeds take hold. They can be left to grow tall and turned in, or cut and used as a regular supply of mulch material.

Some crops are well suited to 'poly-culture' growing systems. In a densely planted mixed species garden, the green manure can become a cover crop or 'living mulch', living semi-permanently under the main crop. Clover or trefoil growing under corn, perhaps with interplanted squash or melon, is an example of a polyculture with an integrated green manure.

Suitable species

Select any species that grows well in your area. Ideally, you want plants that will produce a large bulk in a short time, but do not seed precociously or become rampant. Clovers and fast-growing annual grasses are a common choice. The tables on pages 93–96 contain some suggestions for suitable species.

Other crops

Don't be limited in your choice of green manure crops to those in the table. Any plant that grows well in your garden can become a green manure. Other possible green manure crops include soybeans, chickpeas, sorghum, fenugreek, sunflower,

Turning in green manure

There are three growth stages at which the crop can be turned in, depending on your requirements.

Early-season growth The plant is still in a vegetative growth phase and is rapidly adding new leaf material. The succulent new growth has a high moisture content, so it breaks down quickly. Most humus is rapidly cycled back to crops, so there may be no contribution to longer-term humus levels.

Mid-season growth Plants are starting to form buds and flowers but have not seeded. They may be more woody or fibrous, and break down slower, so they don't provide an immediate boost for subsequent crops.

Late-season growth Most green manure crops should be cut or turned in to avoid seeding. Mature growth is often more difficult to chop or turn under, and breaks down slowly, but can improve soil aeration and contributes longer-term stable humus.

Early-season growth produces soft plant material that decays rapidly. The benefit of the green manure is rapidly achieved and subsequent planting can take place shortly after turning in, say four to six weeks. Turning in early-season growth is generally considered superior green manuring practice. There are good reasons to leave green manure growing for longer in some situations, however, and till it in as a more mature crop. They include:

- using green manure to dry out soggy ground, or when ground is too wet to cultivate
- using green manure to soak up excess nitrogen (for example, in vineyards)
- when longer-term humus input is required (i.e. older, stalkier, higher carbon-content material)
- when maximum input of organic matter is required (for example, the variety Hairy Vetch produces maximum biomass in a growth spurt just prior to flowering).

Leaving winter green manure crops in too long can force a delay in spring planting.

Phacelia, and even leafy vegetables such as spinach and amaranth.

Disadvantages of green manure crops

The main disadvantage of green manures is that while they are growing the land is not available for vegetable production. Seed also has a cost. If not turned in early enough, green manures can lower soil nitrogen levels. And some crops can become a weed problem if left to produce seed.

Green manure crops: legumes

Green manure	Season	Properties	Management
Lupins	Sow in autumn.	Not susceptible to some fungal diseases which may infect peas or beans. Tolerate acid soil. Late-sown crops grow slowly. Susceptible to Fusarium, a fungal disease.	Leave three to four months before turning in.
Lucerne	Lucerne is a perennial plant that retrieves nutrients from deep in soil profile, and open air and drainage channels in soil.	Excellent nitrogen fixer, but takes a long time to establish. Best nitrogen fixation in the second year. Very deep rooted (sources nutrients from deep down). Not suited to shallow soil. Does not thrive unless soil is well drained.	Top growth can be mown and used for mulch or composting.
Field peas	Sow from May through to early spring.	Suitable for summer sowing under irrigation. May be useful to use oats as a 'nurse' crop, to stop peas lodging (to support the peas and hold them off the ground).	Leave three to four months. Best incorporated rather than left as a mulch (pea mulch can become slimy).
Broad bean (fava bean)	Sow in autumn.	A good winter crop that is frost tolerant and will withstand some waterlogging. Tolerates a wide range of soil types.	Turn in preceding a spring-sown crop. Minimum three-month growing period. Turn in when flowers start to drop.
Cowpeas	Sow from October (after danger of frost) to February.	Will tolerate hot weather. Earlier crops produce more growth. Frost sensitive. Prefers good drainage. May require inoculating with 'cowpea' inoculant to fix nitrogen.	Sow summer crops to be turned in at early growth stage.

Green manure crops: legumes (cont.)

Green manure	Season	Properties	Management
Sub clover, white clover and red clover	Sow white clover in autumn (summer- and winter-growing clovers are available from local seed suppliers and garden centres)	Does not produce large amounts of foliage but useful for nitrogen fixation. White clover tolerates acid soil and produces very high nitrogen levels. Grows slowly until established.	May not be killed by mowing.
Vetch		Produces a large bulk and will compete well with weeds. Do not allow to seed. The main variety is Hairy Vetch, which is frost resistant, tolerates acid soil, produces a lot of nitrogen and organic matter and competes well with grasses. On poor ground Hairy Vetch may need some phosphorus fertiliser.	Minimum growing period is ten weeks. May become a weed problem if allowed to seed.

Note: Legumes are sensitive to boron, potassium, sulphur and molybdenum deficiency. They are improved by the addition of appropriate inoculants to ensure that compatible symbiotic organisms are present. Inoculate with commercial preparations or soil from a place where the legume grows well.

Green manure crops: non-legumes

Green manure	Season	Properties	Management
Barley	Sow in autumn in most districts.	Cold tolerant. Winter sowing possible in high rainfall areas. Fibrous root system contributes organic matter.	Leave three months before turning in.
Buckwheat	Sow in early summer.	Needs warm temperatures to germinate. Frost sensitive. Does not produce a lot of biomass but will tolerate low fertility. Accumulates potassium.	Breaks down rapidly if soil is moist.
Canola (also called rape or rapeseed) and other brassica crops (mustard, radish, kale, etc.)	Sow from March to spring.	Will host club root so are unsuitable for use in brassica cropping. Grow rapidly during winter. Canola is very cold tolerant but maximum growth is in late winter and spring. Mustard is a summer crop.	Use as very short-term green manure crops (mustard four to six weeks and canola four to eight weeks). Do not allow to seed because it easily becomes a weed.
Comfrey	Sow any time.	Provides a large bulk of material for turning in, but regrowth from root fragments deep in the soil may make it difficult to eradicate once established.	Best to use as a short-term green manure (six to ten weeks) as mature plants make deep, persistent roots.
Japanese millet	Sow from October to February.	Very fast-growing summer crop. May bolt to seed so mow often to prevent bolting.	Leave eight to ten weeks. Mow Japanese millet several times before turning in, to maximise organic matter production.
Millet	Sow in late winter and spring in most districts.	Fast growing in suitable climates. Does best in warm areas.	Leave in for three months.
Mustard or kale	Spring or summer and autumn to winter varieties available.	Grows very quickly. Not frost tolerant. May produce large quantities of seed if not turned in. Grow several short crops in succession for a very effective 'cleaning' function. Mustard produces allelochemicals when it breaks down, that may prevent germination of weeds. Do not grow prior to a brassica crop as may increase the risk of club root.	Leave in for a minimum of six weeks.

Green manure crops: non-legumes (cont.)

Green manure	Season	Properties	Management
Oats	Sow in autumn.	Will grow well in adverse conditions (e.g. low nitrogen, low soil moisture, cool temperatures). Grows rapidly. Deep root system.	May be used when green or later in growth cycle. Cut or incorporate before seed set.
Rye-grass	Sow in spring and autumn, depending on location (seek advice from garden centre or local expert).	Both annual and perennial rye-grass are rapid growers and provide a good bulk material for turning in. Provides reasonable competition to couch grass.	Minimum growing period four to five weeks. Rye-grass needs to be dug in to 5cm depth to control regrowth.
Cereal rye	Sow in late autumn.	Provides large amounts of organic matter. Good drought resistance. Its extensive growth below the surface helps to stabilise fragile soils. Breaks down more slowly than other cereals. Decay processes suppress weed growth when turned in.	Minimum growth period two to three months.
Sudan grass	Sow in late summer.	Rapid biomass production in hot areas. Tolerates poor drainage.	Grows rapidly in ideal conditions. May be used from six to fourteen weeks of age (older plants are still useful but require more effort to incorporate).
Wheat	Sow in autumn in most districts.	Fibrous root system contributes organic matter.	Use at six to twelve weeks depending on growth.

13. Mulch

'I am always impressed when I remove a straw mulch that has been down for a few months. The improved soil structure from the extra earthworm activity emphasises how effective nature can be when I don't interfere.'
ELIOT COLEMAN, *THE NEW ORGANIC GROWER*, 1989

Mulch suppresses weeds by blocking light to the soil. Mulch will also form a barrier to small germinating seeds or underground plant parts that are trying to reach the light. Any weeds that do germinate will be easier to pull, because the soil under mulch stays loose and moist. Natural mulch also adds organic matter to the soil. Because mulch keeps leaves and flowers clean by reducing rainsplash, there are fewer opportunities to spread soil-borne diseases.

Mulch also moderates soil temperature. In summer, mulch will prevent soil temperatures from getting too hot. Earthworms and other soil organisms stay active longer, and remain closer to the vital feeder roots near the soil surface.

Advantages of mulch

No tillage

Less digging means less hard work. The soil structure is preserved by not lifting and turning the soil, and mulch creates a perfect environment for worms. Most garden earthworms do not naturally move sideways through the soil looking for food. They build vertical tunnels, with feeding chambers off to the side. They stick their anterior or front end out of the hole to locate surface organic matter that they can then pull down into the soil to consume. Not digging preserves earthworm tunnels, and they do the nutrient incorporation for you.

Soil cover

Covered soil stays cooler in summer, reduces evaporation and saves soil water. It also lessens soil compaction from rainfall, heavy watering and foot traffic.

No waiting

If organic materials are only added at the soil surface, you don't have to wait before planting, unless they are strongly allelopathic or growth inhibiting. If uncomposted organic wastes are incorporated, it is advisable to wait at least six weeks for the materials to break down before planting. Until that time, nitrogen will be tied up by the decomposer organisms, and phytotoxic or poison plant chemicals released during the decomposition may retard plant growth.

Soil structure improvement

As plant roots grow down, the influence of the mulch is also extended down into the soil, by the effect of rainfall, earthworms and other animals. This eventually creates an excellent soil structure. The soil will become loose and no digging will be required at all, even for planting seedlings.

Disadvantages of mulch

Contamination potential

When new materials are introduced to the garden there is always a risk of introducing new weed seeds, pests and diseases with them. Movement of mulch is responsible for the introduction of millipedes into many gardens. White conical snails and harlequin bugs often arrive in mulch. Baled straw can harbour slugs and snails, cutworms or other pests.

Prevention of soil warming

Thick mulch will prevent soil from warming early in spring, by stopping the heat of the sun from reaching soil. That can mean later planting or take-off of plants.

Unsuitable for certain plants

Mulching plants that grow from rhizomes and stolons will make vigorous weeds that grow from underground parts even stronger and harder to control at first. The soil may eventually become more friable and easier to dig, but in the meantime the weeds may have taken over.

Avoiding the disadvantages

Many of the potential problems can be avoided if care is taken with selection of mulch materials. Here are a few suggestions:

- Use care when selecting mulch materials. Where possible, locate sources of organic fertilisers, clean well-made compost and organic or spray-free organic material. Use straw rather than hay, as there is usually less weed seed in straw. If buying lucerne hay, enquire about the past performance of the grower (especially about weed contamination), and about the fertiliser and pesticide history of straw, hay, shell and hulls or other waste products. Closely inspect all materials before collecting them. Do they appear to have weed seeds? If in doubt, bring back a little of the potential mulch material, spread it out and water it. After a few weeks, you will see if there is any weed germination, or at least any that will germinate under those seasonal conditions.
- Keep mulch away from plant stems to minimise the risk of collar rot.
- Use controlled irrigation to maintain adequate soil moisture without waterlogging.
- Use simple barriers around young seedlings to exclude pests, such as snails and slugs. Plastic containers with the bottoms removed, or gauze covers, are suitable.
- Pull mulch back in early spring to warm the soil. Old mulch may be composted or loosely stacked and replaced when the soil is warm again.
- Start control of difficult weeds such as couch grass before applying the mulch.

Mulch is a must

Good organic mulch is the best thing you can do for your garden. Compost is often the best material to use as mulch, if you have enough. If not, you can use raw organic matter directly on the soil surface, or a manufactured mulch material, made from organic or synthetic materials. Stones can make a most attractive mulch and are particularly well suited to container growing, courtyards and public areas where organic mulch would blow around and look untidy.

Almost any plant material can be used for mulch. Some materials will last a shorter or longer time, some will be more nutritious, or will have other desirable properties, such as colour to match the landscape setting.

Some of the benefits of mulch, such as

Slugs in mulch

If you are having trouble with slugs in mulch, try the following:

- Place hardwood wood shavings as a barrier around sensitive plants.
- Use shredded bracken, wormwood, southernwood, basil, rue, rosemary or azalea flowers and leaves as a repellent barrier.
- Spray an extract of wormwood, ivy, white hellebore, quassia, lime, garlic and chilli, neem or rotenone directly on feeding snails or as a barrier spray.
- Use alum (aluminium sulphate) or copper sulphate or copper silicate sprays as a barrier.
- Purchase iron chelate baits or copper silicate sprays from a garden centre. Both are permitted inputs under organic certification standards.
- Use beer traps, or any other fermenting substance such as port wine, Vegemite or common yeast. Sink the traps into the ground at 1m spacings between the garden and snail refuge areas, and change them every week or ten days. Added cornflower makes them extra sticky.

protection of the soil surface, apply with almost any organic material used. It is possible to maximise the number of benefits obtained by selecting mulch materials that serve several functions.

Mulch can also help with disease prevention. Apart from general improvement to the health of the plant by removing the stress of drought and temperature fluctuations, mulch forms a barrier between old, disease-infected leaves on the ground and new leaves on the growing plant. Prevention of rainsplash also limits the spread of fungal diseases such as black spot on roses. To make the best advantage of this effect, select mulch that does not retain moisture within the mulch layer, and always remember to push the mulch back a little from the plant stem.

Using mulch

Generally, use the coarser, woody mulches, where a longer life is required, for example, under trees and shrubs. Finer mulches are suited to small seedlings, annual vegetables and flower crops. Finer mulches will need to be replaced more often, but will look better, provide more nutrition earlier, and will not smother small plants.

It is important that soil is moist and warm before the mulch is applied. Some mulch material will absorb a lot of water, and mulch will slow the percolation of water, and may cause dry spots by concentrating and directing water flow. Always remember to push the mulch back a little from the plant stem, to prevent stem rots.

To make mulch last longer:

- use coarsely chipped or shredded native plants, such as eucalyptus, grevillea and melaleuca
- use a thick layer of newspaper, cardboard, plastic or other material such as old carpet under the mulch to help prevent rapid breakdown by soil organisms
- use a thicker layer of mulch.

Suitable mulching materials

Any organic material is suitable for mulching, but some materials may have particular problems and are therefore limited to particular situations.

For annual gardens materials that readily break down are best; that is mulch that breaks down in an annual cycle and can then be replaced. Longer-lasting materials, such as almond shells or pine bark, are best reserved for mulching perennial plants.

Gardens that require warm soil or fine seed beds

Sometimes a mulch garden is inappropriate, such as when soil needs to be warmed by direct sunlight early in the growing season, or small seeds need a fine-tilth seedbed to germinate. If this is the case, then make the mulch garden two or three months in advance. Weeds will be controlled and some nutrients will have been introduced to the soil layers by earthworms. The soil will be friable and in appropriate condition for germinating seeds.

Remove the mulch by raking prior to planting to create a clean seedbed, ready for even small-seeded crops such as carrots and lettuce. Reuse the mulch in another part of the garden, or use it to start a new compost heap.

Seasonal guide

Spring In cool regions rake mulch off annual beds to let the soil warm up. Do not mulch heat-loving plants such as tomatoes and capsicum until the soil is warm. To test the temperature of soil, feel a handful from near the surface early in the morning, before the sun strikes it. You should be able to leave your hand on the ground for three or four minutes without a painful cold sensation.

Summer In hot climates, use light-coloured mulch to reflect the sun and keep soil cool (not suitable for delicate plants). In warm humid climates, organic mulch breaks down quickly and may need to be replenished frequently.

Mulching materials

Material	Notes on use
Animal manures	Must be well aged and preferably well composted
Leaves	Mix with other materials
Lucerne hay	Good nitrogen and useful trace elements; use in infertile and new gardens
Meadow hay	Often contains weed seeds
Pea straw	Contains some nitrogen but beware of weed seeds and cutworm; may get some pea regrowth which is easily removed by hand-pulling
Pine needles	Must be mixed with other materials; do not use thickly on annual plants
Seaweed	Seaweed has good trace elements but breaks down slowly; sea grasses break down quicker and are well suited to annual gardens
Shredded paper	Mix with other materials
Weeds and plant prunings	Mix with other materials; best used after composting
Wheat straw	Often very weed free but has no nutritional value

Autumn In areas with a wet winter, cover annual vegetable and flower beds with mulch in late autumn to reduce soil erosion and leaching of nutrients.

Winter Cover all unused ground with mulch or green manure.

Mulch at a glance

Advantages of mulch

- eliminates many weeds
- retains moisture by keeping the soil moist
- moderates soil temperatures
- less diurnal and annual temperature variation under mulch, and therefore less plant stress
- protects roots and encourages surface feeding
- protects the soil surface from the worst effects of rainsplash, foot traffic and direct drying by the sun, and from wind and water erosion
- adds organic matter and keeps the soil friable
- keeps fruit and vegetables clean from rainsplash.

Advantages of organic mulch

- adds organic matter and creates humus in the soil
- encourages earthworms and other beneficial soil life
- maintains the soil in good structure
- improves moisture retention
- recycles garden and kitchen waste.

Possible disadvantages of mulch

- some materials may be a fire hazard
- may encourage frost damage by preventing radiation of heat from the soil surface, which can heat the air above enough to prevent severe frost
- may prevent the soil from warming in early spring
- may harbour snails and slugs.

Growing your own mulch

A variety of cut-and-come-again plants are used to provide a continual supply of mulch. The fast growth rate of common grasses makes them some of the best candidates for this use. In warm areas the taller growing Barna and Sudan grass produce large quantities of organic matter from a small space. Comfrey also produces large quantities of organic matter from a small plantation. Clovers, peas and vetch are useful because they are legumes and so provide nitrogen. Many of the plants listed in the table on pages 93–96 (green manures) can be cut several times for mulch while they are growing. Some crops, such as sweet corn, provide useful quantities of mulch when the produce has been harvested.

Any other plant that grows easily in your conditions and provides organic matter is suitable for use. Avoid plants that could become a serious weed. Possible annual plants include chickpeas, cowpeas (in warm areas), fenugreek, mung beans, lupins, soybeans, barley, wheat, oats, sorghum, millet, amaranth and sunflowers.

Trees such as *Acacia*, *Albizzia*, *Robinia* (locust tree), *Caeratonia* (carob), *Gleditsia triacanthos* (honey locust)*, *Chamaecytisus palmensis* (tree lucerne, also called Tagasaste)* and *Leucaena**, or shrubs such as *Cajanua cajan* (pigeon pea) or *Caragana arborescens* (Siberian pea tree) also yield useful quantities of nutritious, coarse mulch, or a finer mulch if shredded. They all regrow rapidly from cutting, and can provide a continuing supply of organic

Using living mulch for weed control

The best way to exclude weeds is to cover soil with a dense planting of a hardy competitive species. Once the plants are established they should require little maintenance. Closely planted shrubs and trees may achieve this effect once the canopy closes over, but the technique is more often used with groundcovers. Generally, the groundcover species used should be selected to be self-replacing, or to have a life expectancy of at least five years.

Many plants can be grown as living mulch in close proximity to crops. This system is sometimes called cover cropping, under cropping, or living mulch. It may also be called intimate polyculture. Clovers are ideal as living mulch among vegetables. Common weeds such as purslane (pigweed) and pinto peanut in tropical areas also make ideal ground-hugging living mulch.

matter for many years. They are often used in a system called 'alley farming', where rows of trees are planted to provide shelter for food or fibre crops planted in 'alleyways' between the trees. The trees are harvested on a rotation system to provide mulch for the cropping area. Alley farming provides shelter, refuge area for local biodiversity and mulch in an integrated system.

* Please note that in some areas these plants can become weeds. It is wise to check with your local council or agricultural authority before planting.

14. Quick guide to mulching and mulching materials

Natural mulch materials

Material	Availability	Comments	Hints
Bark	Available from garden centres or timber mills	Some tree bark may be acidic	Larger pieces last longer
Bracken fronds	Cut stems and fronds from local paddocks	Repellent to slugs and snails	Larger pieces last longer
Cardboard	From local supermarkets and stores	Heavily waxed cardboard is unsuitable. Other cardboard is excellent mulch. Cardboard may look untidy, but if used close to the soil and covered with other mulches such as straw or compost, it will increase their life plus weed suppression.	Use around older or established plants
Chipped tree pruning waste	From tree fellers or municipal councils	May harbour some pests	Coarser material lasts longer
Coffee grounds	From restaurants and cafés	High nutrient value. The dark colour absorbs heat.	Mix with sawdust to avoid chocolate smell and prevent mould
Compost	From garden centres, local government or make your own	The best organic mulch. Adds nutrients and organic matter to soil. Attractive dark colour.	Use next to the soil surface and cover with other material. Keep 3–5cm back from plant stems.
Hay	Fodder stores or farms	Leguminous hay crops (lucerne, pea straw) add nitrogen, and decay faster. Grass (and wheat) and meadow hay last longer. Hay may contain weed seeds. Mechanical application is available for larger areas.	Spread one bale out on the ground and water. If many weeds germinate, compost the hay before use.

Natural mulch materials (cont)

Material	Availability	Comments	Hints
Lawn clippings	Home garden and mowing contractors	Valuable nutrients, but if used thickly may cause odour, or excessive heat and matting because of restricted air movement into the soil. Long grass and dry grass are coarser and have less nitrogen.	Use clippings in the compost or spread them thinly. Ideal for use in the vegetable garden.
Leaf mould	Made by composting leaves in autumn	Very useful for water retention and soil improvement. Breaks down rapidly.	Ideal mulch for seedbeds. Very good for ferns and moisture-loving plants.
Leaves	Collect from under trees	Can look untidy if not composted first, and may blow away. Suit native plantings well. Dry leaves from native plants can be a fire risk, so mix with other materials. Fresh green leaves are an excellent source of plant nutrients. Old dry leaves are less nutritious and take longer to break down.	When applying the mulch, water the leaves to stop them blowing away.
Manure	Stables or garden centres	Some nutrient value. Best used after composting. Do not use raw manures on sensitive plants or food plants eaten raw. Breaks down rapidly. Remember that raw animal manures may contain viable weed seeds. To avoid root burn, only use raw manure on actively growing plants. Apply manure or compost tea to any mulch if you want to encourage the rapid breakdown of organic matter.	Compost manure first, or at least leave it to age in a heap for three months. May be used in deeper sheet-composting systems, where it is placed close to the ground and covered with layers of other organic matter.
Mushroom compost	Commercial mushroom farms or garden centres	Excellent dark-coloured mulch with some nutritional value	Pile the compost and let it reheat. It turns into a very dark-coloured, fine-textured material.
Newspaper	Readily available	Unattractive	Spread newspapers thickly and overlap under bark, sawdust or other material for paths or under shrubs.

Natural mulch materials (cont)

Material	Availability	Comments	Hints
Nut shells	Growers and processors	Has some stock feed value, therefore the price is high in areas where feed markets exist. Decomposes slowly (except peanut hulls, which decompose rapidly).	Use 50–60mm deep, with paper underneath for weed control if required.
Paper	Use shredded paper from the office. Commercial paper mulches are also available.	White colour looks untidy in some gardens. Mix with other materials, or use as a base layer under other mulch to increase weed suppression and life of other mulch materials.	Wet paper as soon as it goes down to prevent it blowing away.
Pea straw	Fodder stores or farms	Contains some nitrogen, but beware of weed seeds and cutworm. May get some pea regrowth, which is easily removed by hand.	Excellent for summer vegetables
Pine needles	Pine forest	Must be mixed with other materials. Do not use thickly on annual plants. Suitable for use on native gardens or acid-loving plants.	May inhibit some annual plants as well as weeds. Ideal for azaleas and rhododendrons.
Rice hulls	Rice-growers co-operatives	Finely textured, long life and a good light colour.	Do not apply in windy weather. Wet down.
Sawdust (also wood shavings)	Sawmills and woodwork factories	Excellent mulch for shrubs and for most vegetables. Scatter thinly and do not incorporate into soil because it may cause nitrogen deficiency. Beware of toxic additives such as paint, varnish or polish. Used as a thicker layer, sawdust is the ideal covering for garden paths.	Use the colours (dark red to light) to complement landscaping.
Seashells	Fish processor	Eventually contribute calcium and some trace elements. Makes an attractive mulch in rockeries or around a garden pool.	Use 50–60mm deep. Use paper or plastic underneath.
Seaweed	Seashore. Some commercial seaweed mulches are available.	Excellent mulch, especially kelp (sea grass is of less nutritional value). Kelp provides many minerals and breaks down slower than sea grasses. Kelp may not suit ornamental use.	Do not waste water washing salt off, as most salt is inside the seaweed.

Natural mulch materials (cont)

Material	Availability	Comments	Hints
Stone, pebbles or gravel	Garden centres or quarries	Can be very useful for hardy, drought-tolerant plants, or for alpine plants in rockeries. Colour (e.g. scoria) and texture suit some ornamental uses.	Place a layer of plastic under gravel to prevent weeds, or use a flame weeder. These are available from hire companies.
Straw	Fodder stores or farms	More durable and cheaper than hay. Light colour can suit some situations. Acceptable under fruit trees for controlling weeds and keeping fruit clean.	Light colour suits some landscaping uses. Reflective properties ideal for early spring use.
Weeds	Pull up around the garden	Freely available and contain many useful nutrients, but may also contain seeds. Pull weeds before seed set whenever possible. May not be the most attractive mulch.	Use anywhere. Avoid nutgrass, oxalis and other noxious weeds.
Wheat straw	Fodder stores or farms	Often very weed free, it has no nutritional value.	Use wheat straw bales to retain compost heaps or as a 'white' mulch. Use as a surface layer over less long-lasting mulches such as compost or worm castings.
Woodchips (ornamental)	A variety of light- and dark-coloured chips from garden centres	Excellent for shrubs or flowers	Select from different colours to suit the site.
Woodchips (from native tree pruning)	Local tree fellers or local government	Excellent multi-purpose mulch, usually cheap if delivered in a large load	Lasts longer than sawdust
Wool waste	Garden centres or hardware stores	Manufactured in sheets or round and square 'mats' for use around individual trees and shrubs. Gardeners with access to raw wool waste can also use it for mulching.	Expensive but long-lasting and easy to apply. Ideal weed suppressing mulch for farm trees.
Worm castings	Worm farms or garden centres	Excellent quality mulch, especially where soil improvement and nutrition are higher priorities than weed control (or cover worm castings with a coarser, longer-lasting mulch, such as straw or bark). Excellent mulch for potted plants. Use only when plants are growing.	Use wherever soil improvement and conditioning are required. Excellent for young vegetable and flower seedlings. Short-lived.

Synthetic mulch materials

Material	Availability	Comments	Hints
Aluminium foil	Grocery stores	Very conspicuous. Reflected light will discourage sucking pests such as mites.	Place foil on either side of rows, or cover the whole bed and punch planting holes through the foil.
Black plastic	Garden centres or hardware stores	Excellent for warming soil. Good weed control. Woven plastic weed mats may be better for some uses.	Dispose of plastic after use — do not hoe back into soil.
Carpet	Local tip	Old carpets may have synthetic fibres, and they may have been treated with organochlorine pesticides. May be useful for walkways, or cut into squares for mulching trees.	Do not use on food crops. Ideal for shelter or specimen trees.
Clear plastic	Hardware store	Useful to warm soil rapidly in spring. Will not suppress weeds unless used to 'solarise' in hot weather. (To solarise soil: remove all growth from the soil surface, moisten, dig in edges of the sheet and leave to warm.)	Use for a few weeks in spring prior to planting young seedlings.
Geotextiles (landscaping fabrics)	Manufacturers listed in the Yellow Pages	Some are designed to hold soil together while 'natural' vegetation grows back, therefore they are not ideal for weed control without other treatments.	Use to stabilise slopes and creek banks while groundcovers grow.
Red plastic	Plastic suppliers	Reflective properties are better than black plastic. Can help to discourage mites and other sucking pests.	As for black plastic.
Woven plastic weed mat	Garden centres or hardware stores	Superior to plastic sheeting because the weave allows soil to breathe, and moisture to infiltrate through the mulch.	Use under any permanent plantings.

Further reading

Appelhof, Mary. 1982. *Worms Eat my Garbage*, Flower Press, Kalamazoo, Michigan

Anon. 1992. *Backyard Composting: Your Complete Guide to Recycling Yard Clippings*, Harmonious Technologies, Ojai, California

Bennett, Peter. 1989. *Organic Gardening*, Child & Associates, Frenchs Forest, NSW

Bruce, Maye. 1946. *From Vegetable Waste to Fertile Soil: Quick Return Compost*, Faber & Faber, London. Reprinted as *Common-Sense Compost Making: By the Quick Return Method,* Faber & Faber, London

Bruce, Maye. 1943. *From Vegetable Waste to Fertile Soil*, Faber & Faber, London

Clayton, Sandra. 1994. *The Reverse Garbage Mulch Book*, Hyland House, South Melbourne

Cullen, Mike & Johnson, Lorraine. 1992. *Backyard and Balcony Composting*, Bookman Press, Melbourne

Darwin, Charles. 1881. *The Formation of Vegetable Mould*, John Murray, reissue Faber & Faber

Deans, Esther. 1987. *Ester Deans Gardening Book*, Harper & Rowe, Sydney

Edwards, C.A. & Lofty, J.R. 1972. *The Biology of Earthworms*, Chapman & Hall, London

French, Jackie. 1995. *Soil Food*, Aird Books, Melbourne

Gershuny, Grace. 1993. *Start with the Soil*, Rodale Press, Emmaus, Pennsylvania

Gilbert, Allen. 1992. *No Garbage: Composting and Recycling*, Lothian, Melbourne

Golueke, Clarence G. 1972. *Composting: A Study of the Process and its Principles*, Rodale Press, Emmaus, Pennsylvania

Handreck, Kevin. 1986. *Composting*, CSIRO Discovery Soils Series, Adelaide

Martin, Deborah L. & Gershuny, Grace (eds). 1992. *The Rodale Book of Composting*, Rodale Press, Emmaus, Pennsylvania

Rodale, J.I. (ed.) & Rodale staff. 1970. *Rodale – The Complete Book of Composting*, Rodale Press, Emmaus, Pennsylvania

Rutherford, Peter W. and Lamonda, Mary Lou. 1996. *The Australian Compost and Worm Book*, Apollo Books, Mosman, NSW

Walters, Charles. 1993. *Fletcher Sims Compost*, Acres USA, Kansas City, Missouri

Acknowledgments

It was my father, Jack Marshall, who taught me to compost. He used two systems, the open pile and the in-soil trench method. He also taught me to respect nature and humus, and to garden without chemicals. Thanks for the knowledge and the support and encouragement. Thanks too, Mum, for your continuous support and encouragement.

Many other people have encouraged me in my study of compost and organic growing. I can only mention some. Special thanks are due to David Blewett, Henry Short, Alan Norton, Bill Mollison and Stuart Fraser for starting me out on the right track. Also thanks to Stephanie Goldfinch, Wes Jackson, Alex Podolinski, Sandy Fritz, Chris Alenson and Jonathon Sturm for inspiration and comradeship. Commercial composters Bob Long (Jeffries Garden Soils), Matt Quinn (SA Composters) and Marty Vaher (The Original Green Co) and too many organic gardeners and farmers to name allowed me open access to their compost and growing systems, for photography and information. Special thanks are due to Frank Wolper and Rod May. Thanks also to Lindsay Bock, Amber Laris and Jenny Paterson for encouraging me to stay with organic growing and writing as a career choice. Also thanks to Paul Stephenson, who provided many helpful comments and suggestions on early drafts of the text and many hours of inspirational conversation about organic growing over 20 years. Deb Cantrill provided many useful comments on biodynamic composting methods. Deb and her partner Quentin Jones have willingly shared their knowledge and experience, and make excellent compost at Nirvana Farm, in the Adelaide Hills.

Index